BUCKEYE MADNESS

GOLDEN
OF COLLEGE SPORTS
AGES

BUCKEYE MADNESS

Great Eras in Ohio State Football

WILTON SHARPE

CUMBERLAND HOUSE
NASHVILLE, TENNESSEE

Published by
Cumberland House Publishing, Inc.
431 Harding Industrial Drive
Nashville, TN 37211-3160

Cover design: Gore Studio, Inc.
Text design: John Mitchell
Research/administrative assistant: Ariel Robinson

Library of Congress Cataloging-in-Publication Data

Sharpe, Wilton.
  Buckeye madness : great eras in Ohio State football / Wilton Sharpe.
    p. cm. — (Golden ages of college sports)
  Includes bibliographical references and index.
  ISBN-10 1-58182-452-1 (pbk. : alk. paper)
  ISBN-13 978-1-58182-452-0 (pbk. : alk. paper)
  1. Ohio State Buckeyes (Football team)—History. 2. Ohio State
University—Football—History. I. Title. II. Series.
  GV958.O35S43 2005
  796.332'63'0977157—dc22
                                                              2005022688

Printed in the United States of America

1 2 3 4 5 6 7—10 09 08 07 06 05

*For Mary Margaret, Judith, Jaime, Peg,
and the terrific folks of
Bisbee's Copper Queen Library.
Your help has been and
continues to be invaluable*

*and for Caroline,
thank you, dearest, for your
unending patience and devoted love*

*Howard "Hopalong" Cassady and Hopalong Cassidy
(actor William Boyd)*

CONTENTS

INTRODUCTION

I was born to Buckeyedom in the year 1954. As it turned out, it was an excellent year for my awareness of Ohio State football to kick in. My 10-year-old mind was stirred by the out-of-this-world exploits of Howard "Hopalong" Cassady, the gifted Buckeye halfback then in his junior season at Columbus.

Whatever genius scribe naturally affixed the nickname to Cassady knew at that point in time that there was not a kid on the planet who didn't melt at the name of Hopalong Cassidy, the original man in black, who toted a surefire six-shooter and who, along with his trusty pal Lucky, cleansed the Old West of varmints, riffraff, and desperados. Now a man suited in Scarlet and Gray regalia and toting a laced spheroid accomplished virtually the same thing on a gridiron: Storybook heroes both; iconic giants sharing the big stage.

Lo these many years later, *Buckeye Madness* is a tangible and somewhat nostalgic rendering of the fabled football program at OSU, as told by the players, coaches, assistants, opponents, fans, and members of the media. It's Harley to Hoppy, Kern to Carter, Archie to Eddie, Wilce to Woody, and all the Buckeyes in between. It's humor and history, character and coaches, legendary feet and historical feats. If Ohio State football courses through your veins, this book is for you.

It's all Buckeye.

— W. S.

BUCKEYE TRADITION

People in Columbus will tell you that football didn't start in 1890, when the Buckeyes played their first game, but rather in 1916, when Chic Harley donned the scarlet and gray for the first time. They will tell you that Harley was the "spirit of Ohio State football," the spark that helped build Ohio Stadium and push Ohio State gridiron fortunes onward and upward, until as a gate attraction it has no peer.

Bill Levy
author

Y ou can't overlook how Jim Tressel embraced Ohio State's storied football tradition. When he took over as coach, Jim asked former Ohio State players to write a letter explaining what being a Buckeye meant to them in their lives. Those letters are posted in the locker room, and kids can read them and see what Ohio State meant to a Paul Warfield or a Jim Stillwagon or others before them.

Rex Kern
quarterback (1968–70)

O O O

A noteworthy event took place during the 1897 season. Michigan appeared on the schedule for the first time. The game was played in Ann Arbor, and the better-organized Wolverines won easily, 34–0.

Marvin Homan
former OSU sports information director

Paul Hornung
longtime Columbus Dispatch *sports editor*

"Carmen Ohio" [OSU's alma mater] was written by a bruised and battered freshman football player, Fred Cornell, on the night of October 25, 1902, as Ohio State's hopelessly outclassed football team returned by train from Ann Arbor after a staggering 86–0 defeat at the hands of Michigan. . . . Cornell stretched out on the floor of the train near a warm steam pipe, and as the train chugged along, he started penciling verses to a Spanish chant. By the time the train reached Columbus, he had finished "Carmen Ohio."

Bill Levy

○ ○ ○

The difference between Columbus, Ohio, and anyplace else is, here, there's Ohio State football, *period*. Basketball has done a great job, but you don't have pro sports. It's Ohio State football, it's Ohio State football, it's Ohio State football.

John Cooper
head coach (1988–2000)

I f you don't know about Ohio State foot-ball around here, you musta had your eyes and ears closed for a long time. It's just a way of life around here. You say Ohio State won or lost around here, they know what you're talkin' about, buddy.

Don Hurley
longtime Buckeye fan

O O O

T he 1916 season saw the Buckeyes go undefeated and produce many high-lights: an incredible 128–0 victory over long-time tormentor Oberlin, a first-ever win over Wisconsin, 14–13, and a season ending 23–3 victory over Northwestern to win the mythical Western Conference championship for the first time.

Marvin Homan
Paul Hornung

In the old days after a big Buckeye victory, thousands of students used to put on their nightshirts and hold a "shirttail" parade, marching the five miles from campus to the center of town. With the band playing, they would march through theaters and restaurants singing the "Buckeye Battle Cry" and "Oh, We Don't Give a Damn for the Whole State of Michigan!" Once Al Jolson, the great singer-comedian, was putting on a review in a Columbus theater, when he was interrupted by a "shirttail" group that marched in one door of the theater, up and down the aisles, and out another door. No one tried to stop the parade. If anyone had, the theater might have been left in shambles.

Bill Levy

I t's like seeing *Casablanca*. You could see it 1,000 times but it still excites you. I'd rather dot the "i" before I die than be president. I think it's a greater honor.

Beano Cook
college football analyst,
on Script Ohio

○   ○   ○

B y September of 1919, World War I had ended and Ohio State football was back in high gear. The Buckeyes won six of seven games, losing only the final game to Illinois 9–7 on a field goal in the last nine seconds. The loss cost Ohio State a conference championship and was the only losing game in the entire college career of Chic Harley.

Marvin Homan
Paul Hornung

The epoch 1926 game with Michigan had a serious, near-tragic side. As part of the pre-game pageantry, the Military Department released a series of bombs from a field south of the Stadium. As the bombs exploded, flags were released and carried away by the wind. A sudden, unexpected downdraft forced the final bomb to plunge downward and explode directly over the packed south stands. Two spectators, both women, were burned and required hospitalization. . . . It is no small wonder that promotions of this nature have never been repeated at Ohio State football games.

Marvin Homan
Paul Hornung

THE GOLDEN PANTS

*F*acing an upcoming game with archrival Michigan, Francis Schmidt, Ohio State's innovative head coach from 1934–40, challenged his young Buckeye charges with a time-honored equalizer among men, saying to them, "Those guys put their pants on one leg at a time, the same way you do."

On April 17, 1935, a collection of Columbus businessmen and boosters convened to officially inaugurate the Ohio Pants Club, in honor of Schmidt's "verbal equinox." The group ordained that all future members of Buckeye teams who beat Michigan, coaches as well as players, would be honored at a special banquet with a tiny metal pair of golden football pants replete with an inscription of the historic date and winning score. That longstanding tradition is still alive today.

T he lone loss to Notre Dame in 1935 is one of the most famous games in college football history. Both schools were undefeated and aiming for the national championship as they clashed November 2 at Ohio Stadium. Ohio State led 13–0 after three quarters but the Irish rallied for three fourth-quarter touchdowns [registering the final score with just 30 seconds remaining] to win, 18–13. During football's 100th anniversary in 1969, this game was selected the most exciting contest during the first century of college football.

Jack Park
author

O   O   O

O ver its first century of football, Ohio State won 626 games while losing only 253 and tying 50, a winning percentage of .701.

Marv Homan
Paul Hornung

I t became apparent the war had destroyed a college football dynasty in the making.

Jack Park

on World War II's interruption of the Paul Brown era at Ohio State, which included the school's first national championship, in 1942

○ ○ ○

L es Horvath became the first Ohio State player to win the coveted Heisman Trophy [1944], finishing ahead of sophomores Doc Blanchard and Glenn Davis of Army. Carroll Widdoes was named the coach of the year, the first Ohio State coach to receive this national distinction.

Jack Park

○ ○ ○

W es Fesler's 1949 team [7–1–2] tied Michigan for the Big Ten title and became the first Ohio State team to win the Rose Bowl, defeating California 17–14. This team was greatly strengthened by the addition of sophomore halfback Vic Janowicz, who would soon be recognized as one of the finest all-around players in school history.

Jack Park

SCRIPT OHIO

The incomparable Script Ohio, the Buckeye marching band's legendary halftime rendering of the word "Ohio" in script fashion, is a venerable rite dating back to the 1936 season.

Initially, the band forms a large, triple-stacked Block "O" in the middle of the sideline on the east side of Ohio Stadium. Behind the strains of "Le Régiment de Sambre et Meuse," the lines rotate in opposite directions, before a drum major eventually leads a single line of band members across the gridiron to the west sideline, forming the word "Ohio."

The effect is that of a giant hand writing the word in script. The pièce de resistance is the dotting of the letter "i," sometimes reserved for an honorary guest or dignitary but more often performed by one of the band's tuba or sousaphone players to a roar from the partisan Columbus crowd.

I didn't come here for the security. I came here for the opportunity.

Woody Hayes
head coach (1951–78)

O O O

The Buckeye stickers seen on Ohio State's gray helmets are awarded to a player who makes an outstanding play. It is a merit system that was put in place by Woody Hayes in 1968.

Greg Emmanuel
author

O O O

Of all the traditions we do, that's probably the most important one.

Jason Eberly
OSU student assistant to the
equipment manager, 2002,
on the Buckeye helmet stickers

FAST FACT: During the 2002 national championship season, safety Donnie Nickey earned the most Buckeye stickers in a single week—12. The leaves apparently are passed out somewhat more freely today. Over the course of Ohio State's national championship season in 1968, the high Buckeye leaf earner was defensive back Ted Provost, with 13.

I can tell you this: that Ohio State team, I loved every guy on that team, and I knew that playing in the pros was never, ever going to be the same. With all the tradition at Ohio State and having a coach like we had, everybody cared about each other. My time at Ohio State will always be the fondest of memories. There's just nothing else that could take its place.

Jim Otis
fullback (1967–69)

O O O

This is The Ohio State University. There are no others. What a tradition! I mean, Archie Griffin won two Heismans, and he works right down the hall!

John Cooper

W atching middle linebackers—like Matt Wilhelm—lead the Buckeyes in tackles once was as much of an OSU tradition as Woody Hayes shredding sideline markers and sousaphone players dotting the "i" in Script Ohio.

Jon Spencer

sportswriter,

Mansfield (Ohio) News Journal/
Newspaper Network of Central Ohio

FAST FACT: *Spencer's remark is in reference to the fact that, in five of the six seasons prior to 2002, defensive backs had led the Buckeyes in tackles. The last previous OSU linebacker to lead the team in tackles was Lorenzo Styles, with 132, in 1994.*

O O O

A ll I wanted to do was represent the tradition before me and after me in the best way possible. Ohio State is a living, breathing entity. It becomes a part of you. I am humbled by my experiences there.

Chris Spielman

linebacker (1984–87)/All-America (1986–87)

THE SCARLET AND GRAY

*T*ime and memory tend to be selective when the short list of so-called "greats" is called. Too often, the unnoted player with the heart of a warrior goes unrecognized, lost in the shadow of a Harley, a Horvath, a Cassady, or a Griffin. Look beneath the sheen of the well-oiled machine, and you'll see the might of the worker bees. Without them the Scarlet and Gray could never have generated 29 Big Ten titles and five national championships.

Gomer Jones, the short, stocky Ohio center who later went on to become head coach of Oklahoma, was named on many All-America teams. Jones was considered by many to be the finest lineman in the nation in 1935.

Bill Levy

O O O

Jack Graf, a reserve quarterback all but ignored by Coach Francis Schmidt for two years, was switched by Paul Brown to fullback in 1941, where he ran, passed, and punted his way to Most Valuable Player in the Big Ten—a classic comeback story.

Marvin Homan
Paul Hornung

Gene Fekete, All-Ohio in high school football and basketball, is still considered one of the finest in Ohio State's long and distinguished line of fullbacks. Against Pittsburgh in 1942, he romped for 139 yards, 89 of it on a breakaway TD [OSU 59–19] that still ranks as the longest run from scrimmage by a Buckeye. His school record of 92 points [season] stood until Jim Otis posted 102 in 1968.

Marvin Homan
Paul Hornung

O   O   O

Tommy James, one of the boys Paul Brown had coached at Massillon, starred on defense. But James was also productive on offense, and he would set a conference record in 1942, averaging 11.8 yards per carry for the 20 times he ran with the ball.

J. Timothy Weigel
author

J ohn Borton set a school passing mark by completing 115 of 196 for 1,555 yards and 15 touchdowns in 1952. These marks stood until Art Schlichter broke them as a sophomore in 1979.

Marvin Homan
Paul Hornung

FAST FACT: Borton guided the Buckeyes from 1951–54, sustaining what amounted to a career-ending ankle/leg injury suffered in a 41–20 loss to Illinois in 1953. Though a co-captain in '54, Borton played behind Dave Leggett, who directed Ohio State to a national crown.

○ ○ ○

B rothers Jack and Dean Dugger both played end for the Buckeyes, both were All-America, and both played on undefeated-untied national championship teams. Jack was All-America in 1944 under Carroll Widdoes when Ohio State compiled a 9–0 record and was declared the national civilian champion. Ten years later, Dean earned All-America honors. That season, Woody Hayes's Buckeyes went 10–0 to capture the 1954 national title.

Jack Park

His leadership is just unbelievable. He's the greatest competitor I've ever coached and his spirit is infectious.

Woody Hayes
*on fullback Hubert Bobo of the
1954 national champion Buckeyes*

O O O

Frank Elwood got the quarterback job, even though he had played end the year before. He was not much of a thrower, but he was a straight-A student with the leadership ability Woody wanted. With Elwood calling the shots, the Buckeyes were to turn into the original "three yards and a cloud of dust" outfit. Ohio State finished with 12.8 yards passing gained per game in 1955, still a conference record.

J. Timothy Weigel

I t was a lineman's dream for Ohio State offensive tackle Jim Marshall, who scored both of the Buckeyes' touchdowns. In the first period, he scooped up a blocked punt and rambled 22 yards for his first six-pointer. Marshall returned an interception 25 yards for his second score late in the second quarter to give the Buckeyes a 14–0 lead at the half.

Jack Park

on Marshall's career day as a Buckeye in 1958 against Purdue. Unfortunately, the Boilermakers came back to tie the game at 14–all. Marshall went on to a stellar 20-year NFL career as a defensive end, 19 of those seasons with the Minnesota Vikings' famed Purple People-Eaters of the 1960s and '70s

Guard Bill Jobko, a three-year letterman, never played in a losing Big Ten game. He holds the distinction of being the only Ohio State player to have been a member of three teams which each won the Big Ten title outright.

Jack Park

FAST FACT: Jobko, a member of the 1954 (7–0) and '55 (6–0) Big Ten championship teams, did not play in 1956 when OSU tied for fourth in the conference. He was back again in '57, when the Bucks completed another 7–0 conference run, and was named Ohio State's MVP that same year.

O   O   O

In 1961, Woody Hayes put together an incredible club that included probably the best backfield ever seen in Columbus, even better than the Cassady-Watkins-Bobo-Leggett quartet of '54. All-American Bob Ferguson was the fullback. The halfbacks were Paul Warfield and Matt Snell and John Mummey eventually emerged as the No. 1 quarterback.

J. Timothy Weigel

A first-rate center, Dwight "Ike" Kelley's linebacking in two-way football gained him All-America recognition in 1964 and 1965.

Marvin Homan
Paul Hornung

O   O   O

Here's a trivia question: Who's the only college football player to play for both Woody Hayes and Bear Bryant? Dave Brungard. Brunnie started as a sophomore, started as a junior, then Leo Hayden came in. Brunnie didn't feel that he was going to get a lot of playing time, so he transferred to Alabama and became their starting fullback and a co-captain of their football team.

Rex Kern

O   O   O

Mike Sensibaugh is still the OSU career leader in interceptions with 22.

Marvin Homan
Paul Hornung

H e has a deceptive little run, hasn't he? He's got a deceptive little cut that fools 'em.

Woody Hayes

on quarterback Ron Maciejowski, Rex Kern's backup, who started the 1968 Wisconsin game in place of the injured Kern

FAST FACT: Mace responded with 153 yards passing, 124 yards rushing, three rushing touchdowns, and one TD pass in leading the Buckeyes to a 43–8 victory at Madison. Maciejowski's performance was the second-highest total offense output of the season for the soon-to-be national champs.

○   ○   ○

T he guy that impressed me and one of the guys that made me want to play defense was Timmy Anderson. . . . He was a great player. You know its funny; I got all the publicity, but in some games I graded out at ninety percent and T.A. graded out at ninety-six to ninety-seven percent.

Jack Tatum

cornerback (1968–70), on his fellow Buckeye cornerback. Anderson played from 1968 through '70

I t was just a few plays after the second quarter, I got hurt. I thought nobody could hurt me. We were down near the goal line, and I carried off left tackle or left guard, and I think I got the first down. I'm trying to go eight or nine more yards for the touchdown, just trying to get that extra yardage, and I'm spinning out of one guy, and he had one leg, and I had planted my other foot, and a guy came in from the side, and my knee was—you know—just gone.

Champ Henson
fullback (1972–74),
on the catastrophic knee injury, suffered during
the 37–3 win over TCU in the second game of
his junior season, Sept. 29, 1973, that curtailed
his brilliant OSU career

The first guy I met here was Ken Kuhn. I'm gettin' recruited. I'm sittin' there at this big bar on campus, and they said, "That guy over there at that bar's our captain." I said, "What position?" They said, "Linebacker. I'll introduce you. 'Hey Kuhndog, come over here. This is Tom Skladany from Pennsylvania. He's a punter.'" Kuhn reached over. I thought he was goin' to take my hand, but he took my glass of beer. He drained it, bit it, and chewed the glass. Blood was coming out of his mouth. That's my first impression of Ohio State. I swear to God. He ate glass.

Tom Skladany
punter/kicker (1973–76)/
three-time All-America (1974–76)

Skladany is something!

Woody Hayes

*after punter Tom Skladany's 59-yard field goal
helped beat Illinois 40–3 in 1975. The kick
still stands as the longest field goal
in Buckeye annals*

○ ○ ○

George Hasenohrl was the meanest, toughest guy; another guy who was not the greatest athlete but a guy who made up for it out of brute strength, determination, and self-motivation. He was just a bull, could bend your facemask with his hands. From the old school.

Champ Henson

*on the Bucks' 1972 left defensive tackle
and co-captain*

Realistically, I know I'm in Archie's shadow, but I'm glad I came to Ohio State. I have no regrets. It's better that we were both here at the same time.

Cornelius Greene
quarterback (1973–75)

FAST FACT: It wasn't all Archie Griffin from 1972–75. While Griffin was claiming his second Heisman trophy and garnering All-America recognition for the third straight time in 1975, Greene was voted Big Ten MVP that season ahead of Griffin.

○ ○ ○

Neal Colzie weighs two hundred on the nose and was our outstanding freshman defensive back last year. Definitely. Definitely. Reminds us quite a little of Paul Warfield. Not quite as good yet, but 25 pounds heavier and quick as the devil.

George Hill
defensive line coach (1971–78)

Woody Hayes
during 1972 preseason media day

Art Schlichter set records for passing and total offense from 1978 through '81 that have not been threatened and which represent a forbidding challenge for future Buckeye quarterbacks. Adept at running as well as throwing, Schlichter accounted for 85 career TDs.

**Marvin Homan
Paul Hornung**

O O O

Art Schlichter went from being an all-time Buckeye hero to an afterthought whose name is always accompanied by a nod of the head and three little words, "What a shame"—even in Columbus.

Greg Emmanuel

FAST FACT: Schlichter, the all-time OSU passing leader upon completing his college career in 1981 and the No. 1 draft pick of the Baltimore Colts, developed a betting addiction at Ohio State that deadened a potentially bright future in pro football. For years after departing Columbus, Schlichter's name would recur in the media, usually with a jail term announcement in connection with some gambling offense or bad-check charge.

I can honestly say that Pepper Johnson was the hardest hitting and best linebacker I played against. I didn't like it because we had collisions on nearly every play in practice.

Vaughn Broadnax
fullback (1980–83)

O   O   O

At the end of my career, I had three pairs of gold pants from beating Michigan, and I have to say that beating them up there [1981] was the ultimate.

Mike Tomczak
quarterback (1981–84)

O   O   O

Being the Rose Bowl MVP, I couldn't describe a better ending. I will never forget standing up on that podium after the game with Orlando Pace and the seniors like Greg Bellisari, Luke Fickell, and Mike Vrabel.

Joe Germaine
quarterback (1996–98)/Big Ten MVP (1998)

The greatest game we ever played in was against Michigan at the "Big House" in 1987. I think we were down by three points. I heard Earle calling for the "little guy." He said, "Put him in right now!" When I got the call, I almost threw up my breakfast. He put me in the biggest game of the year, and here I was a freshman. He didn't know if I would hold onto the ball or fumble and let the whole team down. Tom Tupa called the play, and it was a pass. I was the number-three read on the play, so I figured I wasn't going to get the ball. I ran my route to about four yards from the sideline, and I turned and saw the ball coming. It was coming in a hurry, and I was thinking, *Don't drop it!* Seventy yards later, I was in the end zone. It was the greatest feeling in the world to me.

Carlos Snow
tailback/kick returner (1987–89, 1991)

What was best about Craig Krenzel was what was best about the rest of the team. He played the role he needed to play to make us a better football team.

Jim Tressel
head coach (2001–)

○ ○ ○

He's got God's gift. He enjoys doing it.

Michael Jenkins
split end (2000–03),
on versatile Chris Gamble, the first Buckeye in
more than 40 years to start both ways

○ ○ ○

To be able to compete on this level on offense, defense, and in the kicking game, I don't know of a more complete football player in the country.

Glen Mason
University of Minnesota head coach,
on Gamble, who led the 2002 Buckeyes in
interceptions (4), was second in receptions, and
returned punts and kickoffs

I t's incredible today because you only train to go one way. Here's a guy who's not a big individual [6–2, 180], which means he has to be incredible to go both ways at such a high level. If the coach took you out and you didn't play 60 minutes back when I played, you'd think something was wrong. Now you train mentally to just go on the offense or defense. Yesteryear, you prided yourself on being just as good at both. You don't find many Chris Gambles now.

Bill Willis
tackle (1942–44) and Hall of Famer with the Cleveland Browns

I f you throw it anywhere in his area, he's going to come up with the big play. To have a guy that tall and that athletic, I couldn't imagine having that kind of talent.

Ben Hartsock
tight end (2000–03),
on teammate and split end Michael Jenkins

O O O

M ichael Jenkins is one of those guys that you don't even know is there because he's working. You love those kinds of guys. Some guys wear you out; they want you to know they're there. Mike is just a steady guy and a big-play guy.

Jim Tressel

H e's been like the sparkplug in our car.

Troy Smith
quarterback (2003–),
on high school and now Buckeye teammate
Ted Ginn Jr., whose four punt returns for
touchdowns in 2004 set an Ohio State and
Big Ten record and tied the NCAA mark for
most TD punt returns in a single season,
only the third player in NCAA history
to achieve that standard

O O O

W hen Ginn is in full flight, he appears to be the fastest player in the Big Ten, possibly the country.

The Sports Xchange
Ohio State team report

O O O

I try to make something out of nothing.

Ted Ginn Jr.
wide receiver/punt returner (2004–)

BUCKEYE
CHARACTER

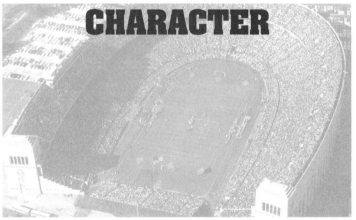

Greatness can be found in simplicity.

Rex Kern

O O O

The Old Man [Woody Hayes] used to say, "Let the scoreboard do your talking." And that's what we did.

Nick Roman
defensive end (1966–67, 1969

When the Super Sophs came in, they were different. They had a hop in the way that they walked. They were not terrified of Woody.

Jim Otis

on the star-studded sophomore class of 1968 who helped lead the Buckeyes to the national championship

O O O

You can't measure cohesiveness or heart; it's easy to overlook. But those intangibles are important strengths that we [OSU] developed throughout the 2002 season. Our positive attitude helped us through tough times, and I think Jim Tressel fostered that demeanor.

Rex Kern

on the 2002 national champion Buckeyes

We just stick together; we're a team out there. We never give in or point the finger at anybody. We just keep fighting and find a way to win.

Michael Jenkins

O O O

I'm more of a quiet, laid-back guy who gets things done and leads by example. You can celebrate after the game.

Michael Jenkins

O O O

The stuff that happened in the 1997 Penn State game wouldn't have happened on our teams. No way. Those guys [the '97 Bucks] were 12-up and started celebrating, and then Penn State comes back and kicks their butts. You would never see *us* smiling. When somebody was down and we had our foot on their throat, we pushed harder on it.

Nick Roman

When I walked on that field and I looked at you, it wasn't *if* I was gonna whup your ass, it was *how* I was gonna whup your ass.

Jim Parker
guard (1954–56)/All-America (1955–56)/
Outland Trophy winner (1956)

O O O

We had six, eight, ten running backs and wide receivers we could've given the ball to. That's a challenge for the quarterback, as well as for Woody. When you spread that all out, you develop closeness and you develop people who rely on other people. Everyone shared in the glory.

Rex Kern

Not only did he make me into a good football player, but he gave me something that I could take away from the game—the tools to be successful later. Whether guys liked him or disliked him, played or didn't play, they all left with the same tools.

Tim Fox
safety (1972–75)/All-America (1975),
on Woody Hayes

O   O   O

He once earned two oak leaves—the OSU equivalent of the Silver Star—for hauling six and seven Wisconsin tacklers with him on respective plays, and he once carried the ball 21 times after suffering a broken nose.

Alan Natali
author,
on Champ Henson

I had total reconstruction. Lost a ligament, I mean totally, just snapped off. I still couldn't believe it: "This ain't happening." Just like I didn't believe the other thing [his quick, dynamic success as a scoring, short-yardage fullback] wasn't happening. Right when I'm believin' that it is, this happens [the knee injury], and I ain't believin' this, either. After they did the reconstruction, I said, "I'm gonna play in the Rose Bowl." They said, "That's 12 weeks away. Nobody can do that." And I did.

Champ Henson

O   O   O

Nothing in this world is worth having if you don't have to work for it. Whatever you get feels better when you know you got it yourself.

Woody Hayes

Y ou should try and do the right thing, but you can't be a role model to every kind. You want to talk about heroes, there's a couple of old guys around here, who went away in 1941, didn't come home until 1946. Four or five Christmases away from home. Come home, work like dogs all their life. Never hear 'em complain. Those are heroes. Some guy, because he scores a few touchdowns or hits a few home runs, I'm supposed to look up to him? As far as being a role model for what's right and what's wrong, it has no correlation at all.

Champ Henson

There's too many positive things out there for me to get carried away with the negatives.

John Cooper

O   O   O

The difference is belief.

Tim Anderson

defensive tackle (2000–03)

O   O   O

I don't want to hear any excuses for why we can't win at Ohio State. I use this old country saying: "Don't worry about the horse goin' blind, load the wagon and pull the line." Get the job done. We don't need to worry about injuries, or the weather, or the pre-game meal, or the bus ride, or the officiating. Don't look for reasons why you're not successful, just make it happen.

John Cooper

Every time something happens to me, it happens for the best. I'm never down, because no matter how bad it is, something's gonna work out. Nothing can happen that's so bad that you can't keep going on.

Tom Skladany

○　○　○

I believe it was the four best years of my life. I learned the most as a person that I could have anywhere. I had the most fun, and I acquired some of the best friends of my life. I learned what it was like to be down and what it was like to be successful. I certainly learned how to win.

Bruce Elia
linebacker/fullback (1972–74)

I t didn't really matter to me when I was named All-Big Ten and All-America. It really didn't. I never really liked individual honors like that. I took more pride in receiving Buckeye leaves and being named the team's "Defensive Player of the Week." I had been voted captain for my junior and senior years, and to be recognized by your peers like that, no All-America team can match that. It's how you play in the eyes of your peers and what type of person you are for them . . . that's the stuff that matters.

Pepper Johnson
linebacker (1982–85)/All-America (1985)

BUCKEYE HUMOR

It was popularly believed that Woody Hayes's teams didn't even know a ball could be thrown, but like a guy who didn't find out about girls until he was 40, Woody's team went slightly wild when they did learn the pass was legal. Getting beat on the pass by Ohio State is like getting mugged in church by a statue.

Jim Murray
Los Angeles Times *columnist,*
after Ohio State's 1974 Rose Bowl victory
over Southern California

A Jim Tressel-designed offense is usually as cutting edge as that choirboy's necktie-and-sweater-vest ensemble he favors on game day.

Jon Spencer

O O O

I t's the best win of the day.

Jim Tressel

referring to the Buckeyes' heart-stopping,
last-minute, 10–6 win over Purdue to keep
their 2002 Big Ten and national championship
hopes alive

O O O

I t's not every day you hear burly carni-vores being asked if they like tortilla chips.

Jon Spencer

on the post-game media questioning following
Ohio State's 14–9 win over Michigan to wrap up
the 2002 Big Ten title and a spot in the
Fiesta Bowl against Miami for the
national championship

We've got the best damn band in the land. Now we've got the best damn team in the land.

Jim Tressel

after OSU's victory over Miami to claim the 2002 national championship

○ ○ ○

I always said three things can happen on a pass. I was wrong. There's a fourth thing: You can get fired!

Woody Hayes

quipping to an after-dinner crowd sometime after his dismissal as head coach. The reference is to Hayes's timeless quote that three things can happen when you pass, and two of them are bad

○ ○ ○

Murder, yes. But never divorce.

Mrs. Woody Hayes

when once asked if she ever considered divorcing her husband

T he only thing that could have stopped him was the Pacific Ocean.

Lou Holtz

defensive backfield coach (1968),
to an exasperated Woody Hayes, who had
asked Holtz at halftime of the 1969 Rose Bowl
game why O. J. Simpson had run 80 yards
for a touchdown

O O O

I don't have a ticket. I'm the new coach.

Paul Brown

head coach (1941–43),
to an Ohio Stadium security guard who, failing
to recognize Brown, had halted the OSU
mentor as he attempted to enter the stadium.
Ultimately, Brown was reduced to having
to throw pebbles at the Buckeyes' locker room
windows to get the attention of someone who
would go talk to the guard

I t was a wild, hot game and we won, and [the coaches] said we played like crap. Every game we played that year, we played like crap. We won another one, we played like crap.

Jim Stillwagon
middle guard (1968–70)/All-America (1969–70), on the OSU coaches' not-too-well-disguised attempt to keep the young 1968 Buckeyes from believing their press clippings, as they moved toward a national championship

Bo Undercover

The day before the 1975 battle with Michigan at Ann Arbor, Woody Hayes displayed the prowess, in his mind at least, of a super sleuth that would have evoked the envy of agent Maxwell Smart or even the great Sherlock Holmes himself.

As the Buckeyes were taking their lunchtime meal in a University of Michigan dining room, Hayes stunned his players by suddenly rising from his seat, tapping his glass for the attention of the facility's Maitre d', and promptly ordering him to eject the attractive Michigan coeds serving his players, who were then replaced as waiters by the cooks in the back.

"Men," stated Hayes proudly, "Bo [Schembechler] infiltrated our lunchroom today. He put these girls in here to get your mind off the game, but I caught it. I just want to let you know the kind of guy you're playin' against tomorrow."

The Buckeyes, to a man, dying of laughter on the inside, nodded their serious support of Hayes extraordinary action.

The strategic warfare of the legendary Woody-Bo duels had reached a new level.

Francis Schmidt had so many plays that his quarterback in 1936, Tippy Dye, had to carry play cards in his helmet. In one game, the helmet was knocked off his head and the cards were strewn across the field. Players on the opposing team were quick to help Dye pick up the cards.

Bill Levy

○ ○ ○

Schmidt outlined the entire game plan on the seat of one of his player's pants. A cloudburst came along early in the game and completely washed away the plays, game plan, and all.

Bill Levy

on an incident during Francis Schmidt's coaching career at TCU prior to his stint in Columbus

L es, you told me that football trophy of yours was really something special, but it turns out that everyone we know has one.

Mrs. Les Horvath

*after seeing Heisman Trophies while visiting
with her husband at the homes of friends
Mr. and Mrs. Tom Harmon and Mr. and Mrs.
Felix "Doc" Blanchard. Harmon and Blanchard
won the prestigious award in 1940 and '45,
respectively. It seems that Mrs. Horvath,
unaware of the trophy's importance, had been
waging a domestic campaign to rid the
Horvath home of the presence of the well-
known football statue, since it vied with her
distinct decorative ideas for the living room*

BUCKEYE LEGENDS

When somebody starts in with that bullshit about football players being dumb jocks and animals, I have just two words for them: Rex Kern.

Woody Hayes

THE GREAT WES FESLER

In the long annals of Ohio State football leading up to the 1940s, the only player to rival the great Chic Harley in stature was three-time All-America end Wes Fesler.

The six-foot, 180-pound Fesler played aggressively on both offense and defense for the Buckeyes from 1928 through 1930, but his magnificent athleticism flowed over into other sports as well, and he became one of the early prototypes of the three-sport athlete.

In basketball, he starred as a three-time All-Big Ten player during the same years that he was garnering All-America recognition on the gridiron.

In addition, Fesler played baseball while at OSU. His proficiency on the diamond is best described by a victory over Illinois during his junior year, in which he belted three homers—two of them grand slams—plus two doubles, driving in all eleven runs against the Illini.

M ost who saw him play came away with the feeling that he was the nation's best football player in 1930.

Bill Levy

on legendary Buckeye end Wes Fesler

O   O   O

F esler went on to a coaching career that took him to Harvard, Wesleyan of Connecticut, Princeton, and Pitt before returning him to Columbus. And even the fine teams he turned out from 1947–50 could never overshadow his own exploits in three sports from 1928–30.

J. Timothy Weigel

O llie Cline was voted the Big Ten's Most Valuable Player in 1945, the third Buckeye so honored in five years [Jack Graf in '41, Les Horvath in '44]. Cline's 229 yards rushing in the Pitt game survived as an OSU record until Archie Griffin ran for 239 against North Carolina in 1972.

Marvin Homan
Paul Hornung
on the Buckeye fullback (1944–45, '47)

O O O

I 'm not sure that there has ever been a greater offensive guard. He was everything an offensive lineman should be.

Woody Hayes
on Jim Parker

O O O

I f you can find one play that I played at Ohio State where I loafed, you bring it to me and I'll pay you for it.

Jim Parker

THE OHIO STATE UNIVERSITY

Jim Parker

WILLIS TRACKS DOWN
BUDDY YOUNG

Tackle Bill Willis was the first Ohio State football player to be named to both the college and pro football halls of fame.

Countless times during his days in Columbus, the great tackle displayed uncanny athleticism for a lineman, but Willis saved his most impressive performance for the 1944 game against Illinois at Cleveland's Municipal Stadium, where he would later star as a member of the Cleveland Browns.

Before a capacity crowd of 83,627—the largest wartime crowd to attend an athletic event—Willis awed the throng with one unforgettable play.

Illini halfback Buddy Young, reputed to be the fastest man in college football, had broken away for what appeared to be a sure touchdown, when the lightning-quick Willis, who was also a sprinter on the Buckeyes' track team, chased him down from behind and tackled him, helping to preserve a 26-12 OSU victory.

A fter the 1960 season, fullback Bob Ferguson won All-America honors and Tom Matte, a fast, elusive, and dangerous runner who played both halfback and quarterback during his career from 1958–60, was voted the team's most valuable player. Ferguson averaged an impressive 5.3 yards per try.

Marvin Homan
Paul Hornung

O O O

B ob Ferguson won All-America honors in 1960 at fullback and he figured to be even better in 1961. Both halfbacks were sophomores but had unusual ability. The left halfback was a lean, fast, graceful athlete named Paul Warfield, and the right halfback was a strong, powerful youngster, Matt Snell.

Marvin Homan
Paul Hornung
on the "All-Pro" Buckeye backfield of 1961

FAST FACT: *Though Ferguson also was a consensus All-America selection in 1961, the quintessential three yards-and-a-cloud-of-dust fullback never matched the impact of Warfield and Snell in pro football, playing just one season with Pittsburgh.*

I had the endurance and ability to do what I did in the pros because of Woody Hayes. I can't give him any more credit than that, and this is a guy that gave me ulcers in college.

Tom Matte
*halfback/quarterback (1958–60) and 12-year
NFL veteran with the Baltimore Colts*

O O O

He's the best quarterback I've seen in the Big Ten in 10 years. He's taught me some things about quarterbacking.

Woody Hayes
on Tom Matte

S peedy, graceful Paul Warfield played in 1961, '62, and '63. He played tailback the first two years but was moved to wide receiver as a senior. Difficult to tackle in the open field because of his speed and change-of-pace running style, he led Ohio State in pass receiving in '62 and '63. Warfield enjoyed a brilliant Hall of Fame career in the NFL with the Cleveland Browns and Miami Dolphins as a wide receiver.

Marvin Homan
Paul Hornung

O O O

W e used Paul Warfield part of the time on defense, you know. Put him on Wisconsin's Pat Richter once, a darn good end up there in Madison, and Warfield just ate his lunch. Richter made five yards.

Woody Hayes

Matt Snell, one of Ohio State's 1963 co-captains, was a starter three consecutive seasons at three different positions. Snell started at right halfback in 1961, defensive end in '62, and fullback in '63.

Jack Park

O   O   O

Rex Kern often concealed the ball so well opponents despaired of finding it until the play had been completed. Always imaginative, his ball-handling likewise was faultless.

Wilbur Snypp

Bob Hunter

authors

O   O   O

Rex Kern's ball-handling often confused the NBC television camera crew.

Jack Park

*on the Buckeye quarterback's Rose Bowl
MVP performance, New Year's Day 1969
against Southern California*

THE OHIO STATE UNIVERSITY

Rex Kern

Determined Jim Otis led the Buckeyes in rushing from 1967 through 1969 and was the 1969 All-America fullback.

Marvin Homan
Paul Hornung

O   O   O

Defenders found John Brockington difficult to stop. Especially in 1970, when the rampaging fullback gained over 1,000 yards and made All-American.

Marvin Homan
Paul Hornung

O   O   O

I remember [defensive coordinator] Lou McCullough saying about Jack Tatum, "This is the next Jim Brown."

Jim Roman
center (1966–68)

FAST FACT: Tatum, with impressive offensive credentials and a huge upside, started out on offense for Ohio State as a freshman before being switched to defense, where he became an All-American in the Bucks' secondary from 1968 through 1970.

We didn't have too many egos. Like the guys that should have had egos—like Rex [Kern]; he was as down to earth as anyone else. And the thing I liked about Rex, he wasn't a prima donna. He'd get knocked out and get up and try to come back the next play and run the same play he got knocked out on.

Jack Tatum

O O O

I tell you the best football player I ever coached was Jim Stillwagon. Because he worked every day from his freshman year until the day he left. He gave you a hundred percent. I mean he really worked.

Lou McCullough
defensive coordinator (1963–70)

While checking into my dorm as a freshman, I saw all these all-staters and All-Americans. I was all-nothing. I thought, *What am I doing here?* Rex Kern and Jack Tatum were seniors and part of a national championship team, and here I was a freshman going up against them in practice. I questioned myself. One time in practice we called a blitz and I broke free and was just about to tackle Rex Kern, when all of a sudden John Brockington came out of nowhere and hit me so hard I thought he broke my sternum. But I healed, and I figured out I could play with these guys. It was somewhat of a turning point for me.

Randy Gradishar
linebacker (1971–73)/All-America (1972–73)

John Hicks is our best offensive football player. If he's not the best damn tackle in the country, I'd like to see the man who says he's not. We'll take 'em both out in the woods and, by God, we'll see who comes out of there!

Woody Hayes

○ ○ ○

A teammate, frustrated by chasing Cornelius Greene in practice, groused, "It's like trying to tackle a fart."

Alan Natali

○ ○ ○

I have found that being a quarterback under Woody Hayes, you need all the faith you can get.

Cornelius Greene

By Cornelius Greene's fourth game, opposing coaches were complaining that they couldn't find anyone athletic enough to emulate him during drills. Greene became the most versatile and exciting quarterback in college football. He brought to football the skills and flare of basketball [he'd been a three-sport All-American in high school]: deft ball handling; creative, instantaneous decision-making; balletic footwork.

Alan Natali

O   O   O

He has the same type of quickness as Jack Tatum. He's as fast as anyone we've got; he's got great hands and he's got great ball sense.

Dick Walker
secondary coach (1969–76),
on safety Tim Fox

O   O   O

You just do what you do best, and what I did best was hit people.

Tim Fox

A nytime you can be the MVP of the team, that is special, but to be MVP of a team that includes the greatest player in the history of college football is something unbelievable.

Cornelius Greene
who, in addition to his selection as team MVP, was voted Big Ten MVP in 1975 ahead of Heisman Trophy-winning teammate Archie Griffin

○   ○   ○

I used to see Pete run by guys and they used to jump on his back. And I don't blame them, because you hit him head on, and you have some work to do.

Archie Griffin
tailback (1972–75)/ Heisman Trophy winner (1974, '75), teammate of running back Pete Johnson with the NFL's Cincinnati Bengals, as well as at OSU

P ete Johnson and Archie Griffin remain the only Buckeyes to gain 1,000 yards in the same season.

Alan Natali

O O O

H e was such a physiological anomaly [his thighs measured 29 inches] that Pete Johnson's coaches became obsessed with his weight and conditioning. Players, coaches, and trainers crowded around to watch Johnson weigh himself. To make him feel less conspicuous, Woody Hayes even climbed on the scale first. The coach wanted Johnson to play at 240, but after practice and some extra laps one sultry August day, he had gone from 255 to 256. Hayes surrendered, calling Johnson "the ideal blend of speed and power."

Alan Natali

E very time I ran the ball, I was trying to hurt somebody. I wanted respect; I wanted to make them respect me. It's another thing Woody drilled into me.

Pete Johnson
fullback (1973–76)

O   O   O

T om Skladany, three-time All-America punter from 1974–76, is the only specialty team player in Ohio State history to be selected a co-captain. Skladany averaged 42.7 yards on 160 career punts and also holds the school record for the longest field goal, a 59-yarder at Illinois in 1975.

Jack Park

FAST FACT: Skladany's honor as OSU's only special teams captain (1976) was matched in 2004, when the Bucks elected kicker Mike Nugent as one of the team's three captains.

Before my junior year, I developed a new practice routine. I went home and punted around a nine-hole golf course. I punted from the side of the number one tee; I would jog, pick it up, stop, and punt again. I would punt it to the green, go pick it up, and jog to the next tee. For 300 yards, you would have six punts, and all that running in between.

Tom Skladany

O O O

Chris Spielman is college football personified.

Earle Bruce
head coach (1979–87)

O O O

I've followed Ohio State football for 40 years and I like what I see out of Orlando Pace. He's a big fellow with good speed, good balance, and he really blocks well.

Jim Parker

O rlando Pace is a great athlete. There's not much difference in the role he plays and the role I played. He's the go-to guy on that line, just like I was. You have to have a person who wants to be the guy the team goes to when the game is tough. You need that force.

John Hicks
tackle (1970, 1972–73)

O O O

O rlando Pace has the whole package— the height, the size, the speed, and the athletic ability, but most important for a great offensive lineman, he has recover ability.

Jim Lachey
tackle (1981–84)/All-America (1984)

O O O

O rlando is the man. He's the most amaz- ing athlete I've ever seen on the offen- sive line. If you want a tough yard, just run behind Orlando. That's what we did all season.

Eddie George
tailback (1992–95)/
Heisman Trophy winner (1995)

God, is he good. He's a special player.

Chuck Stobart
assistant coach, receivers (1995–2000),
on wide receiver Terry Glenn

○ ○ ○

I've been telling you all year long . . . he'll make you forget Joey Galloway.

John Cooper
on Terry Glenn,
after Glenn's record-setting 253 receiving yards
in the 54–14 blowout of Pittsburgh, Sept. 23,
1995. Glenn also scored an OSU record-tying
four touchdowns in the romp

○ ○ ○

He just totally shuts down the other team's top receiver. When you look at his side, you know he's going to take care of his guy and make it just ten on ten out there.

Damon Moore
strong safety (1995–98),
on two-time All-America cornerback
Antoine Winfield

LEGENDARY COACHES

There are three things that can happen when you pass, and two of them ain't good.

Woody Hayes

O O O

I never saw a man make a tackle with a smile on his face.

Woody Hayes

John Wilce thought of himself as God Almighty. He never admitted that Chic Harley was the spirit of Ohio State. He got to the point where he didn't recruit football players. He felt they should come to him.

Anonymous sportswriter
*on the Buckeyes' coach from 1913
through 1928*

O O O

Sam Willaman was colorless, and in the ethic that had taken possession of men's minds, that was even worse than not winning championships.

J. Timothy Weigel
*on the OSU head coach from 1929–33,
who fashioned a .695 winning percentage
and twice beat Michigan*

O O O

It has been said that everyone in Columbus has two jobs—his own and coaching the Ohio State football team.

Bill Levy

Francis A. Schmidt was an advocate and master of the multiple offense. It was not unusual for one of his teams to display seven or eight formations and have 300 plays in its repertoire.

J. Timothy Weigel

*on OSU's innovative head coach
from 1934 through 1940*

○   ○   ○

He had a great, great offensive mind.

Sid Gillman

*end (1931–33)/assistant coach
under Schmidt (1938–40)/
Pro Football Hall of Fame head coach*

○   ○   ○

Were he alive today, Schmidt would be considered way ahead of his time. At the time he arrived in Columbus, he was light years ahead of his time.

Elmer Layden

*one of the legendary Four Horsemen
of Notre Dame and head coach of
the Fighting Irish from 1934 through 1940*

THE ECCENTRIC
FRANCIS SCHMIDT

Ohio State's 14th head coach, Francis A. Schmidt (1934-40), was a study in nonstop creativity, motion, and, well, oddness.

It wasn't uncommon to see the main Buckeye mentor in a restaurant completely absorbed, hunched over a napkin or scribbling on the back of an envelope, diagramming new plays as he ate dinner.

His obsession carried over to when he was driving an automobile, sometimes roaring around town in second gear, so preoccupied with his X's and O's that he would forget to shift the transmission.

But the best Schmidt tale involves a visit to a gas station, where he elected to remain with his car while it was being serviced. The attendant raised the car eight feet into the air on a lift, and Schmidt, focused on his play diagrams and oblivious to the fact that the vehicle had been elevated, began to step out of the car. Only a timely yell from the alert mechanic spared the Buckeye mentor a perilous fall.

Paul Brown was much more sound fundamentally than Schmidt.

Jack Graf
fullback/quarterback (1939–41)/
Big Ten MVP (1941)

O O O

A groundswell developed for 32-year-old Paul Brown, the "Miracle Man of Massillon," to succeed Francis Schmidt. Brown had transformed a downtrodden, debt-ridden Massillon high school football program almost overnight into a perennial state champion. From 1932 through 1940, his Tiger teams won 80, lost eight, and tied two against strong opposition, both in-state and out-of-state, and hadn't been defeated in the last four seasons.

Marvin Homan
Paul Hornung
on Paul Brown's ascendancy to the Ohio State
head coaching job in 1941

O O O

I like 'em lean and hungry.

Paul Brown
on what he looked for in a player

T he excitement of Paul Brown football stemmed from smooth execution. His OSU teams quickly and convincingly demonstrated why he came by the nickname "Precision Paul."

Marvin Homan
Paul Hornung

O   O   O

I 'm convinced that clean living and trying hard will win.

Paul Brown

O   O   O

P aul Brown's years at Ohio, and the year after he left, were confused by World War II. Players came and went from campus to campus, wherever their units were training. Eligibility rules were in constant flux and, generally, coaches had less to work with than they had before the young men started to go off to fight.

J. Timothy Weigel

I was better satisfied as an assistant than I have been as head coach.

Carroll Widdoes

head coach (1944–45)/assistant coach (1941–43, 1946–48),
upon tendering his resignation to the OSU athletic board, after posting a 16–2 record and the highest winning percentage in Ohio State football history (.889) in his two seasons as head coach, including guiding the undefeated 1944 "national civilian champions" team. Widdoes asked for and received his request: to return to his old chores as backfield coach, citing an intense dislike for public appearances in addition to the huge pressures of the head coaching job

Woody Hayes had the ability to make a good player great, a great player a superstar, and a superstar the greatest.

Jim Stillwagon

O O O

He magnetized, hypnotized me. He could take a guy with a wooden leg and make him run a hundred-yard dash.

Jim Parker
on Woody Hayes

O O O

You were afraid of him as a freshman, you hated him as a sophomore, liked him as a junior, and loved him as a senior.

Tom Skladany
on the Hayes phases

On the trip up to close the season against Michigan in Ann Arbor, a sportswriter noticed that one of the two team buses was jammed and the other was empty. A player explained the phenomenon. Pointing to the empty bus, he said, "Woody's in that one."

J. Timothy Weigel
*on the close to Hayes's first season
at OSU, in 1951*

○   ○   ○

I despised him. Most of us did.

Bo Schembechler
*OSU assistant coach (1958–62)/
21-year Michigan head coach,
when he first met Woody Hayes,
as an offensive tackle at Miami University
of Ohio playing under Hayes,
then the RedHawks' head coach*

○   ○   ○

I'm not trying to win a popularity poll, I'm trying to win football games.

Woody Hayes

Woody would get the team so fired up when they run out of that locker room, and they're all singin' that Ohio State battle cry—'Drive, drive on down the field'—you could go out there and defeat Napoleon's army.

Jim Parker

○ ○ ○

During his sometimes-volatile tenure as OSU's coach, Hayes ripped up his own hat, threw his wallet, threw his attaché case, stomped on his own watch, crushed his own glasses [until his hands bled], threw down markers on the field, threw water coolers, threw coffee, threw play cards, threw telephones . . . Basically, if it wasn't nailed down Hayes probably threw it.

Greg Emmanuel

In what has to stand at the height of a temper-laced career, in a state of unadulterated rage, Hayes once even punched himself in the face—with both fists, cutting his cheek with his own 1968 championship ring.

Greg Emmanuel

○ ○ ○

When you're a freshman, you're standin' there at practice, and you see someone fumble, and Woody bites his hands until it bleeds. You know what I'm saying—bleedin'. That freaks you out. Then, someone throws an interception, and he starts beatin' himself in the face. Black and blue, fat lip. You're sayin', "This guy's committed." You realize how bad the guy wants to win, and you want to help him win so he doesn't hurt himself.

Tom Skladany

He was not the irascible person he was often portrayed to be. He was a man of great compassion, who was a tremendous positive influence on the players he coached.

Joe Paterno

*legendary Penn State head coach,
on Woody Hayes*

O O O

One of Woody's downfalls was he would outthink himself. Woody was predictable when it was close.

Jim Stillwagon

O O O

The alumni never won a football game in their life; they don't block that well. You win with good kids you believe in . . . and who believe in you. How the hell do you think I've been around as long as I have? I never paid a damn bit of attention to the city or the alumni or anybody else— except myself!

Woody Hayes

If people don't criticize Woody Hayes, there's something wrong with them. I walked by the mirror Sunday and almost took a swing at him.

Woody Hayes

○   ○   ○

Woody Hayes isn't crazy enough to get committed . . . but if he ever was, they'd never let him out.

Forest Evashevski
former Iowa head coach

○   ○   ○

People often ask me why most of my hair is gone and all of it is white, even though I'm still a pretty young man. I tell them, it's because I had to spend my college days playing for Woody Hayes and now I have to spend my career days coaching against him.

John Pont
*former head coach at Yale,
Indiana, and Northwestern*

THE OHIO STATE UNIVERSITY

Woody Hayes

Woody Hayes was only the third coach in OSU history to go through a season without defeat [1954]. John Wilce in 1916 and Carroll Widdoes in 1944 were his only predecessors.

J. Timothy Weigel

O O O

Whenever you go through an undefeated season, you are lucky.

Woody Hayes

O O O

Somebody once said that football is a lot of clichés, and I believe every damn one of them.

Woody Hayes

O O O

Eliminate mistakes in football, and you'll never lose a game.

Woody Hayes

A football team improves more between the first and second games than any other time of the season.

Woody Hayes

O O O

His success has turned Columbus into a football citadel that ranks as high as any in the pigskin pantheon, and that includes South Bend, Tuscaloosa, or anywhere else.

J. Timothy Weigel
on Hayes

O O O

Don't worry, you're only the fifth quarterback that Woody has given an ulcer to.

Doctor Bob Murphy
to Cornelius Greene

O O O

We never apologize for winning.

Woody Hayes

He did more for Big Ten football than any coach in our conference's history. I owe Woody a lot . . . we all do.

Bo Schembechler

former Michigan head coach and longtime Hayes arch opponent during the "great 10-year war"—the robust rivalry between Ohio State and Michigan during the years 1969–78

O   O   O

They can call me anything, just so they don't call me a "nice old man."

Woody Hayes

O   O   O

A lot of times I go out and I talk to kids and stuff and I'll be telling them something and it'll hit me: Man, you sound just like Woody. It's things that he told us, points that he made to us.

Jack Tatum

Woody Hayes was Big Ten football.

Bo Schembechler

O   O   O

Around here, Woody was like Elvis. You know, there was no mistake: "That's Woody Hayes." All the other coaches looked like insurance salesmen, but Woody's Woody.

Champ Henson

O   O   O

We knew when we were there that we were playing for a legend. Not after. We knew right then and there.

Tom Skladany
on Hayes

e loved him, and we hated him.

Ken Kuhn
*linebacker (1972–75),
on Coach Hayes*

○ ○ ○

I have a temper. I've had it all my life. I have a lot of regrets, but we all do. Do you expect me to go around crying over spilled milk?

Woody Hayes
*following his infamous slugging of Clemson
linebacker Charlie Bauman in the
1978 Gator Bowl loss to the Tigers*

"I WILL NOT BE YOUR COACH NEXT YEAR"

Those words fell onto stunned ears, as Ohio State icon Woody Hayes informed his squad on a chartered flight returning to Columbus the day after the 1978 Gator Bowl in Jacksonville, Florida, that he would no longer be their coach.

In that fateful game, Hayes "crossed the line" one final time, punching in frustration a fully uniformed Clemson Tiger player, middle guard Charlie Bauman, who had just ended a potential OSU game-winning drive with an interception of an Art Schlichter pass.

Following the incident, seen by millions live on network television, OSU officials met and voted to relieve Hayes of his head coaching duties. He never coached again.

The Woody Hayes era (1951–78) closed with a school-record 205 victories, three national championships, 13 Big Ten titles, having produced 58 first-team All-Americans and 131 All-Big Ten selections.

I felt terrible for Woody the night that happened with the kid from Clemson, but they couldn't keep him after that. It was a sad way for him to end what was one of the all-time greatest careers in college football. I'll tell you something a lot of people don't know: The kid he hit was roommates with our owner here, Jim Speros, and Jim told me that Woody became very close with that kid's family, good friends. That was impressive.

Tom Matte

O O O

I think if Woody would've had his druthers, he would've liked to have died on the battlefield. He would've liked to have had a heart attack out there right in front of the 95,000 people.

Tom Matte

It's a challenge to follow Woody Hayes, but I guess I'm a guy who goes for great challenges.

Earle Bruce

O O O

It's tough when your only defeat of the year is by one-point.

Earle Bruce

*following the deflating 17–16 loss to USC
in the 1980 Rose Bowl, after going 11–0
and being ranked No. 1 in the nation,
beating Michigan, and claiming the Big Ten
championship outright during the 1979 season*

O O O

Sound defense is the first ingredient of winning football.

Earle Bruce

Football is really a 10-yard game. Ten yards, three downs, three-and-a-third yards a down, and you keep the ball. Then you play strong defense and you win the football game. That's what it was supposed to be all about. Football was supposed to be a toughness sport. Now they're making it a doggone basketball game. Always taking shots from mid-court.

Earle Bruce

O O O

Earle was old school. He was very prepared, very disciplined, and very organized.

Mike Tomczak

on Earle Bruce

I guess I always will be a Buckeye at heart.

Earle Bruce

in deciding to remain at Ohio State after anguishing over an attractive offer to coach at the University of Arizona following the 1986 season. Ironically, Bruce was fired without apparent cause by university president Edward H. Jennings the following year after a 6–4–1 season

◯ ◯ ◯

In my opinion, there's two, four, five percent of the people who are very, very vocal, very negative, and anti-anything. They were anti-Woody and they were anti-Earle. Those coaches were fired. Ohio State doesn't have a great image nationally for the way they've treated coaches. It's impossible to please everybody here.

John Cooper

Some people say you have to be dead or be gone to be appreciated around here, and that may be true. I'm not gonna tell you that I haven't had some times when I figured, "I need this?"

John Cooper

O   O   O

Recruit the best players you can, give 'em everything you possibly can to make 'em successful, and let 'em play. Sometimes you win, sometimes you lose. Sometimes you kick that field goal that wins the game, sometimes you don't get the breaks.

John Cooper

O ne thing nobody could fault was John Cooper's ability to recruit Ohio's best talent. During the Tennessean's tenure, OSU became a veritable NFL factory— smoking and coughing out some of the most highly touted footballers in the professional game. In the 1990s, while Cooper suffered from the I-can't-beat-Michigan blues, Ohio State University was the nation's number one producer of NFL-bound talent. During Cooper's watch, 15 OSU players were taken in the first round of the NFL's annual draft.

Greg Emmanuel

Woody Hayes was a great football coach, but when you think about it, why did he have to be so mean? You don't have to be mean to the media. You don't have to berate the coaches and players. You can still be nice to people and get their respect.

John Cooper

○ ○ ○

Sometimes if you give us coaches a chance to think, we foul things up.

Jim Tressel

○ ○ ○

Any hard-fought victory is a good one. I'd rather learn lessons that way than after hard-fought losses.

Jim Tressel

○ ○ ○

Champions go undefeated in the month of November.

Jim Tressel

He had given us something called "The Block 'O' of Life," which outlined goals of family, football, and education. What struck me was that he wasn't just a football coach—he wanted to know everything about you.

Cie Grant

linebacker (1999–2002),
on Jim Tressel

O O O

Pouring a bucket of ice water on this guy brings his temperature up.

Rusty Miller

Associated Press sportswriter,
on Jim Tressel

O O O

Earle Bruce always says that if the Ohio State coach wins against Michigan he can walk down the main streets of Columbus. If he loses, he'd better walk the back alleys.

Jim Tressel

3–1 against the Buckeyes' archrivals,
through 2004

THE GREAT OHIO STATE RUNNING BACKS

I f you want to know why coaches get ulcers, sit around and think about Archie Griffin carrying the football for three more years.

Bob Blackmon
former Illinois head coach

C hic Harley weighed 162 pounds when he came to the Ohio varsity after a year on the freshman team. Fast as the wind and a superb drop-kicker and passer, he is the man who replaced the cow college with the football juggernaut. . . . Harley made Ohio State a national power and made Columbus something more than the capital of Ohio.

J. Timothy Weigel

○ ○ ○

T he best piece of football machinery seen in the vicinity this year.

Walter Eckersall

*turn-of-the-century University of Chicago
football immortal and later a writer
for the* Chicago Tribune,
*on Chic Harley, who in 1916 became the first
sophomore All-America since Eckersall in 1904*

Most of his running was wide. If you got him past the line of scrimmage, it was ten to one he'd go for a touchdown. On wide runs, he would put his hands on top of an enemy's helmet and pivot right around him. He would go at less than full speed as long as he could. Guys would tackle both legs and he'd still get away. The football was rounder in those days and Harley could throw it like a baseball. He was a quadruple threat. He could pass, placekick, punt, and run.

Russ Needham
former sports editor,
Columbus Dispatch

THE OHIO STATE UNIVERSITY

Chic Harley

H arley was an almost invincible runner, the spirit of Ohio football.

Paul Leach

Chicago Tribune News

O   O   O

T he impact of Charles W. "Chic" Harley, a sophomore halfback from Columbus East High School, on Ohio State football was beyond imagination.

Jack Park

O   O   O

C hic Harley was named to the Walter Camp All-America team for the third time [in 1919]. He won letters in four sports at Ohio State and without question ranks as one of the greatest athletes in the history of the University to this day.

**Marvin Homan
Paul Hornung**

FAST FACT: Harley scored 201 points during his OSU career (1916–17, 1919), including 23 touchdowns, 39 PATs, and eight field goals. He led the Buckeyes to their first two Western Conference (forerunner of the Big Ten) championships and played in only one losing game during his career, a 9–7 loss to Illinois in his final game.

H arley is one of the greatest players the country has ever seen. He is an excellent leader, shifty, fast and one of the best open field runners in years.

Walter Camp

the Father of American Football and originator of the All-America teams, who selected Harley for the honor in 1916

O   O   O

I n 1950, the Associated Press conducted a poll of 391 sportswriters and broadcasters to determine the greatest college football player of the first half of the twentieth century. Chic Harley tied for ninth place.

Richard Whittingham

author

The 167-pound Les Horvath, although fulfilling a demanding schedule in dental school, never missed a practice and played a team-leading 402 game minutes in 1944. A quarterback in the T formation and tailback in the single wing, he accounted for 924 yards rushing, 344 yards passing, led the team in scoring [72 points], and keyed the defensive secondary.

Marvin Homan
Paul Hornung

FAST FACT: Horvath was OSU's first Heisman Trophy winner, gaining the award in 1944. He was also selected to all 13 All-America teams that same year.

○ ○ ○

Horvath's non-statistical contribution meant as much. He was in every sense a coach on the field, steadying his talented freshman backfield mates; calling signals, calling defenses; building team confidence and lending inspirational leadership, particularly at crunch time.

Marvin Homan
Paul Hornung

THE OHIO STATE UNIVERSITY

Les Horvath

P laying his final season in a time when the quality of college football was of uncertain caliber, Horvath was a good, steady performer, but not the explosive type like Howard Cassady. Cassady did not have the passing skill of Horvath, nor did he have the all-around ability of Vic Janowicz.

Bill Levy

O O O

L es Horvath won the Heisman Trophy in 1944 over Army's Mr. Inside [Doc Blanchard] and Mr. Outside [Glenn Davis]. He also was named Big Ten most valuable player and claimed the Nile Kinnick Trophy and the Christy Walsh Trophy to cap a brilliant career that placed his name alongside Chic Harley and Wes Fesler in the Ohio Pantheon.

J. Timothy Weigel

I saw Tom Harmon play a few games in college, but Vic Janowicz was the greatest college player I ever saw. After his senior year, he went to three postseason All-Star games. He was the MVP as a quarterback in one of the games, the MVP as a tailback in a single wing in another, and the MVP as a halfback in the third game.

Jack Buck

longtime St. Louis Cardinals broadcaster and onetime sportscaster for WCOL in Columbus

○ ○ ○

It was like when I played tag as a kid. I didn't want anyone to catch me.

Vic Janowicz

*tailback/safety/punter/kicker (1949–51)/
Heisman Trophy winner (1950),
on his elusive ways as a running back*

A nyone who saw Victor Janowicz play football knew at first glance that this was no ordinary player. He was a hard, shifty runner. He could throw the football with supreme accuracy. He could punt, and when he kicked off from his own 40-yard line the ball often went sailing out of the end zone, more than 70 yards away.

Bill Levy

O   O   O

J anowicz played baseball in high school but never in college. He signed with the Pittsburgh Pirates after college as a catcher and played a few games in the big leagues before he went on to a career in the NFL with the Washington Redskins.

Jack Buck

I t's the finest bit of open field running I've seen since the days of Chic Harley and Illinois' Red Grange.

Lew Byrer

sportswriter,

on Vic Janowicz's dazzling 61-yard punt return against Iowa in 1950, which helped propel OSU to an astronomical 83–21 win, the most points ever scored by the Buckeyes in a Big Ten Conference game. On the afternoon, Janowicz scored two touchdowns, passed for four more, kicked ten extra points, kicked off three times beyond the end line, and recovered two fumbles. He played barely any of the second half

O   O   O

I n 1967, the Big Ten would publish its history and refer to Janowicz in 1950 as "Mr. Unbelievable."

Pat Harmon

writer

THE OHIO STATE UNIVERSITY

Vic Janowicz

Howard "Hopalong" Cassady

I n 1952, Howard "Hopalong" Cassady was only in the freshman year of what was to become an incredible OSU career. Hoppy scored three touchdowns in his first varsity game as the Bucks beat Indiana 33–13 to start the season.

J. Timothy Weigel

O   O   O

H e sees beyond the first tackler to the second and third and sometimes the fourth. Howard Cassady isn't one of those ballplayers that runs 40 yards to pick up 10. He knows what that goal line is for. He can make his cuts at top speed without missing a step. He can take a tackle and roll with it to keep going if it isn't a solid tackle.

Esco Sarkkinen
end (1937–39)/All-America (1939)/
longtime assistant coach-scout (1946–77)

Howard Cassady is the greatest college football player I have ever watched.

Wilfred Smith

former sports editor, Chicago Tribune,
January 1956

○ ○ ○

Not only are you the greatest football player I've ever seen, but also, off the field, you're just a little better than the greatest.

Woody Hayes

on Howard "Hopalong" Cassady

○ ○ ○

The remarkable thing about Hop is that he does it, and does it, and does it again!

Woody Hayes

○ ○ ○

An electrifying player with a quick change of pace, Hop's dip of a hip could fake a rival defensive back out of Ohio Stadium.

Cooper Rollow

writer

hile working at WCOL they told me to go see a running back at Central High School in Columbus. I went and saw this red-headed kid running all over the field and said to myself, "He'll never do that in college." How wrong I was. It was Howard "Hopalong" Cassady.

Jack Buck

O O O

e's the most inspirational player I have ever seen.

Woody Hayes
on 1955 Heisman Trophy winner
Howard "Hopalong" Cassady

ike Harley and Cassady before him, Archie Griffin had starred in Columbus high school football and was expected to follow their lead into a Scarlet and Gray uniform.

Marvin Homan
Paul Hornung

O   O   O

here has probably never been so sensational a debut in the 50-year history of Ohio Stadium as that of 18-year-old Eastmoor grad Archie Griffin.

Paul Hornung

former Columbus Dispatch *sports editor*

O   O   O

y most memorable game in all of football is the North Carolina game my freshman year.

Archie Griffin

on his first full game as a Buckeye freshman,
a 29–14 victory over North Carolina in 1972,
in which he rushed for 239 yards, setting a new
Ohio State single-game record

rchie Griffin became the only two-time winner of the Heisman Trophy. He also established a college record rushing for more than 100 yards in 31 consecutive regular-season games and established an NCAA career rushing record with 5,177 yards [since broken]. His career rushing average of 6.13 per carry is still an NCAA record.

Jack Park

FAST FACT: Griffin is also the only player ever to start four Rose Bowls.

O   O   O

he 31 straight 100-yard games are my greatest football accomplishment. You talk about a pounding. It took a lot of pounding to get that done.

Archie Griffin

Archie Griffin

Arch gets hit almost every play, and when he has the ball, he gets hit about four times.

Woody Hayes

on Griffin's senior season as a "marked man," en route to his second Heisman

O   O   O

I have them sitting on my bookcases, at the top, so every time I want to get one down, I have to climb a ladder to get it. It's a great feeling to be in with that group of people who have won the Heisman, and I'm honored to be the only one to win two, but it's still a team award for me.

Archie Griffin

Archie Griffin is the greatest back I've ever seen or coached. He's also the most popular player we've ever had, by far. In fact, we value Archie's attitude more that his football ability, which is saying something, because he can do everything.

Woody Hayes

O   O   O

I expect that sometime, somewhere along the line, somebody is going to win twice. Having that title, "Two-time Heisman Trophy-winner," is special to me. It's very, very special to me, but I don't worry about having to share it with someone. I can always say, "I was the first."

Archie Griffin

K eith Byars did it all. He is so sudden, so versatile, and has everything a good back needs. He is equal to any college back I have been around.

Mike White

Illinois head coach,

after Ohio State came from 24 points down to beat the Illini, 45–38, in 1984, thanks to Byars's school-record 274-yard rushing effort and record-tying five touchdowns

○ ○ ○

I n 1983, Keith Byars rushed for 135 yards and caught four passes totaling 120 yards against Purdue to become the first Buckeye to top the century mark in both rushing and receiving in the same game since Ray Hamilton in 1949.

Jack Park

K eith Byars had a remarkable season in 1984, leading the NCAA in rushing, scoring, and all-purpose yards. He rushed for a school record 1,764 yards and scored 24 touchdowns.

Marvin Homan
Paul Hornung

FAST FACT: Byars also was named consensus first-team All-America in '84 and was runner-up in the Heisman Trophy balloting to Boston College's Doug Flutie. A broken bone in his foot, sustained in preseason practice in 1985, curtailed further record-breaking for Byars at OSU.

O O O

R unning the ball is a two-way street at Ohio State. The linemen block for me and I run for them.

Keith Byars

Eddie George is in a class by himself.

Lawyer Milloy
*University of Washington All-America safety,
after George became the first player in OSU
history to rush for 200 or more yards three
times in his career, carrying 36 times for 212
yards and two touchdowns in the Buckeyes'
30–20 win over the Huskies, Sept. 16, 1995*

O O O

That is the first time I heard the chant, "Eddie, Eddie!" at the stadium. It was overwhelming.

Eddie George
*on his record-setting effort
against Washington in 1995*

O O O

Big No. 27, wow.

John Cooper
on Eddie George

I remember looking up at the scoreboard. I had 188 yards at the half and thought, "Whoa, this is getting out of control." I broke the record sometime in the fourth quarter. I really had no idea how many yards I had [314 on 36 carries]. It was that night that I heard people talk about me and the Heisman Trophy in the same sentence.

Eddie George

*on his Heisman Trophy-winning performance
in the 41–3 conquest of Illinois in 1995
that broke Keith Byars's previous Ohio State
single-game rushing record of 274 yards*

O   O   O

Eddie George was just spectacular. Eddie was just a nightmare.

Lou Tepper

*Illinois head coach,
after George's 314-yard performance
single-handedly crushed Illinois, 41–3,
in 1995*

THE OHIO STATE UNIVERSITY

Eddie George

139

I've been in this business for 35 years, and Eddie George has the best work ethic of any player I've ever been around. He set the standard here. He was the heart and soul of our team.

John Cooper

O O O

Eddie's not flashy. He's the old work-horse. He puts in eight hours a day, works hard, and goes home.

John Cooper
on George

O O O

How do we replace him? Well, with more than one guy. It's going to be impossible to find one guy to do all the things Eddie did. I could draft running backs for the next 30 years and I may never draft another Eddie George.

Floyd Reese
Tennessee Titans GM

H ere was a kid who'd been a celebrity since he played midget ball. Maurice was like an eight-year-old Jim Thorpe. I told him straight up: I'm not getting in the line of people who tell you how great you are. I'm getting in this real short line of people who tell you what you're doing wrong.

Thom McDaniels

Clarett's high school coach
in Warren, Ohio

O   O   O

M aurice Clarett rushed for 175 yards and three touchdowns in his debut [Aug. 24, 2002], added 30 yards in receptions, and didn't get stopped once in the backfield on his 21 carries. Enrolling at OSU early so he could participate in spring drills obviously paid off for the Youngstown native.

Jon Spencer

He's not a freshman to me. The kid works hard. The benefits he reaps on Saturday he deserves because he works hard Sunday to Friday to get better. He's a great back.

Matt Wilhelm

*middle linebacker (1999–2002),
on freshman tailback sensation Maurice
Clarett, after his 230-yard rushing performance
against then-10th-ranked Washington State
in 2002*

○ ○ ○

Pure and simple, he was the difference in that cardiac-arresting 14–9 win over the Wolverines, just as he has been the single largest reason for Ohio State's finest season in 24 years. Seldom if ever has a team gone into a national championship game with its chances for victory linked so directly to the performance of a teenager.

Austin Murphy

*Sports Illustrated,
on Clarett*

MAJOR MOMENTS

Wes Fesler concluded one of the most brilliant careers in Ohio State grid history against Illinois at Champaign. The Buckeyes had been unable to score against Illinois in their 1927, 1928, and 1929 meetings. But Fesler put 12 points on the scoreboard in the first quarter of the 1930 meeting and it was enough for a 12–9 triumph over the Illini.

Bill Levy

I t was Mardi Gras, the World Series, and the end of prohibition rolled into one.

J. Timothy Weigel
on the pre-game atmosphere in Columbus prior to the legendary Notre Dame-Ohio State game of 1935

○ ○ ○

I t may take an act of Congress to stop 'em.

Anonymous reporter
on Ohio State's first-half explosion against Notre Dame in 1935, in which the Buckeyes led 13–0 into the fourth quarter before eventually losing 18–13

FAST FACT: Both teams had entered the contest unbeaten. For many years, it was hailed as the greatest college game ever played. Trailing 13–12 with less than two minutes to play, Notre Dame attempted an on-side kick, which failed. The Buckeyes, however fumbled the ball back to the Irish on an off-tackle sweep, opening the door for a final Notre Dame tally by way of William Shakespeare's pass to end Wayne Millner, in one of the historic defeats in OSU annals.

○ ○ ○

18-13. Three fourth-quarter touchdowns for the Irish. Ohio State was the best team in the country for three quarters.

J. Timothy Weigel

T he contest had been nicknamed the "Bad Water Game." Many Ohio State players became ill from the drinking water on the train to Madison, Wisconsin, on Friday. By Saturday afternoon, nearly half the squad was unable to play at full strength.

Jack Park

*on the 1942 loss to Wisconsin,
the only blemish on the Buckeyes'
first national championship season*

O O O

Q uarterback John Borton's five touchdown passes and end Bob Grimes's four touchdown catches against Washington State in 1952 are Ohio State single-game records which stand yet today.

Jack Park

THE SNOW BOWL

It was Columbus's worst blizzard in 37 years. Yet the Ohio State-Michigan game of 1950 would be played, producing one of the great classics in college football history, as six to eight inches of snow fell during the contest.

The Wolverines, without ever gaining a first down, claimed the conference crown and a Rose Bowl berth with a 9–3 win, attempting nine passes and completing none. In addition to the record 45 combined punts by both teams, there were 10 fumbles.

The Wolverines amassed a total of 27 yards to OSU's 16 and blocked two Vic Janowicz punts that yielded a safety and a touchdown.

A debatable decision to punt by Ohio State head coach Wes Fesler just 47 seconds before the end of the first half resulted in the blocked punt by Michigan that was recovered for a touchdown—ultimately the winning margin in the game.

A few weeks later, under great duress from unforgiving fans and the press, Fesler resigned.

THE OHIO STATE UNIVERSITY

1950 Snow Bowl

H aving the ball today is a liability.

Bennie Oosterbaan

*legendary Michigan All-America end
(1925–27)/head coach (1948–58),
on the legendary Snow Bowl game of 1950*

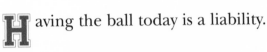

I t was a game played by heroes. They had to be to play football on a day like this. The conditions were the worst in the world. Unless you were down there on the sidelines, you have no idea. The boys would come out with their hands blue from the cold. It's amazing that the boys played as well as they did.

Wes Fesler

*head coach (1947–50) and three-time
All-America end (1928–30),
on conditions in the historic Snow Bowl
loss to Michigan in 1950. The early winter
snowstorm produced 28 mile-per-hour winds
and 10-degree temperatures*

In the famous [or infamous] 9–3 Snow Bowl loss to Michigan in 1950, Vic Janowicz kicked a 38-yard field goal despite swirling snow and treacherous footing. In a survey of sportswriters years later, it was voted one of the greatest feats in American sports.

Marvin Homan
Paul Hornung

FAST FACT: Accounts of the length of the Janowicz field goal vary, with most saying 38 or 27 yards. The New York Times detail of the game lists the ball on the 22 before the kick.

○ ○ ○

I could see the goal posts but not the stands behind. Conditions weren't so bad in the first half. If it'd been the second half, it would've been impossible.

Vic Janowicz
on his legendary field goal in the 1950 Snow Bowl against Michigan

FAST FACT: In that game, Janowicz lofted 21 punts for a 35-yard average, including one kick of 60 yards. But Michigan's Chuck Ortmann punted 24 times for 723 yards. Both still stand as Big Ten marks.

CASSADY'S INTERCEPTION
AGAINST WISCONSIN

Before an overflow crowd of 82,636 at Ohio Stadium in 1954, the Buckeyes hosted Wisconsin, rated No. 1 in the nation.

With the Badgers holding a 7–3 edge in the third quarter, Wisconsin quarterback Jim Miller dropped back to pass. Spotting an open receiver, Miller threw deep into Ohio State territory.

But Buckeye defensive back Howard "Hopalong" Cassady had deliberately lured the Wisconsin QB into thinking his man was open. As Miller released the ball, Cassady made his move, stepping in front of the receiver at the Ohio State 12 and making the pick before beginning his journey upfield.

Crossing midfield and racing for the east sideline, Cassady cut sharply to the inside as a Badger tackler approached. But the Wisconsin player was no match for the quick and speedy Buckeye, who dashed the rest of the way untouched for a storied 88-yard interception return.

That go-ahead touchdown spurred Ohio State on to a 31–14 upset victory that thrust the Buckeyes into the national spotlight.

THE OHIO STATE UNIVERSITY

Howard Cassady's 88-yard interception return vs. Wisconsin in '54.

I t was the most spectacular play in 20 years of football in our stadium.

Woody Hayes

*of Howard Cassady's momentum-changing
88-yard interception return for a touchdown
against Wisconsin in 1954*

O   O   O

T he January 1, 1955, Rose Bowl will be remembered for two things: 1) The game was played in a downpour from start to finish, and 2) for the remarkable play of Buckeye quarterback Dave Leggett, who handled the ball on 80 plays from scrimmage under atrocious weather conditions without a fumble.

**Marvin Homan
Paul Hornung**

FAST FACT: Swampy field conditions left the Rose Bowl turf badly torn up, exposing a muddy morass on which the game was played. The 20–7 win over Southern Cal capped an undefeated season for the Buckeyes, giving them their first national championship since 1942.

T he greatest one-man exhibition of ball carrying since the legendary Bronko Nagurski of Minnesota.

Anonymous veteran sportswriter

on OSU fullback Bob White's memorable performance against No. 5-ranked Iowa in 1957. Trailing 13–10 midway through the final quarter in a game that would decide the Big Ten championship, Ohio State marched 68 yards for the winning score behind the Herculean efforts of White, who carried the ball on seven of eight plays of a 68-yard OSU drive in which he personally gained 66 yards. White's carries went for four, nine, twenty-nine, six, ten, three, and the final five yards for the winning touchdown

ne of the day's most spectacular plays was executed by Paul Warfield. On a counter play right, the fleet halfback turned the end, cut back upfield, faked Michigan's safety off his feet and raced 69 yards for the second-longest scoring run from scrimmage in the series' history.

Jack Park

Fast Fact: OSU blew out the Wolverines, 50–20, in 1961 for the Buckeyes' 400th all-time victory.

○ ○ ○

t was definitely interference. It was the worst-called play in the history of college football.

Woody Hayes

on the controversial interception by Michigan safety Thom Darden in 1971 in the closing minutes of OSU's 10–7 loss to the Wolverines, in which Hayes felt strongly that an Ohio State receiver had been interfered with

A closer look at one play in the first half perhaps gave OSU faithful and the players a glimpse of things to come. The Buckeyes had the ball, fourth-and–8 on the SMU 41. Hayes called for the punt team to take the field, and as it did, Kern waved off the unit. He ultimately scrambled for 15 yards and the first down, but not without first deflecting solid hits while twisting and turning and keeping his feet. It was a classic scramble, the kind of effort for which Kern would be known through three seasons.

Steve Greenberg

author,
on the commanding confidence of sophomore
quarterback Rex Kern in his first varsity game
for the Buckeyes, a 35–14 win
over SMU in 1968

I took it on the dead run. It was so wide open down the sideline all I had to do was catch the ball and run it in.

Ted Provost

*cornerback (1967–69),
on his 35-yard interception of a Mike Phipps
pass for a crucial second-half touchdown
against No. 1-ranked Purdue in 1968 that
propelled the Buckeyes to a 13–0 victory along
the road to their eventual national
championship. Provost's play is one of Ohio
Stadium's most celebrated touchdowns*

Woody called a hitch pass to Jan White. It was the 99-Hitch. I remember going back [in the pocket] and seeing the linebacker sitting on Jan, and I knew it was not going to work . . . So I thought, *I'm in trouble here.* And then it was like a truck went through there; the line opened up. The defensive back was in the end zone, and he stayed in the end zone. I went right to his feet.

Bill Long
quarterback (1966–68),
on his 14-yard scoring run against top-ranked
Purdue in 1968, considered by many to be one
of the most important touchdowns in OSU
history, that solidified the Buckeyes'
13–0 victory

There was no panic. I went into the huddle and told the guys, "We better start playing football." I think O. J.'s run did more to wake us up than to excite his teammates. I thought Woody did a great job not coming out of his game plan after O. J. scored.

Rex Kern

on Southern Cal's 10–0 start in the 1969 Rose Bowl, highlighted by O. J. Simpson's electrifying second-quarter 80-yard touchdown run. The Buckeyes buckled down, however, ultimately prevailing, 27–16, for their first national championship since 1957

W oody made us sign papers and put down what we were going to do to beat Michigan. Then he read them all to the team. That's how intense that game was. I mean, we could not lose that football game. That was not in the agenda, no way.

John Brockington
*fullback (1968–70),
on the enormity of the 20–9 win over Michigan
in 1970, avenging the demoralizing upset
by the Wolverines the previous year
that robbed the Buckeyes of a second
consecutive national crown*

O O O

I have never had a team more ready to play. I've got to feel this was our greatest victory! This makes up for what happened last year.

Woody Hayes
*after his Buckeyes' 20–9 revenge victory
against Michigan in 1970*

I've never seen such determination and courage as our boys showed in those tight moments.

Woody Hayes

on the Buckeye defense's two memorable goal-line stands against Michigan in 1972 that preserved a 14–11 OSU win. Michigan coach Bo Schembechler twice forewent point-blank-range field goals that would have given the Wolverines a tie and outright possession of the Big Ten title

O   O   O

It's the greatest victory we ever had; the greatest game we've ever, EVER played!

Woody Hayes

following the 42–21 Rose Bowl triumph over Southern California in 1974

We knew we had to pass to beat Southern Cal. We passed a lot of the time we practiced out here, and that's where I got my confidence. I think after Coach Hayes watched me, he really had confidence in me to throw in clutch situations. During the season, we usually ran when we needed yards bad.

Cornelius Greene

on his Rose Bowl MVP performance that stunned USC in the Buckeyes' 42–21 1974 victory in Pasadena. The Trojans had expected and prepared for the typical OSU offensive approach under Hayes, running the football. Greene crossed up Southern Cal, completing six-of-eight passes for 129 yards and rushing for one touchdown

R ay Griffin's interception was one of the really significant plays in the history of the Ohio State-Michigan series. He was outstanding on defense with fourteen tackles including ten solos.

Jack Park

Griffin's key pick in the closing minutes of the 1975 Michigan-OSU game at Ann Arbor set up fullback Pete Johnson's third score of the game, earning the Buckeyes a 21–14 victory and a trip to the Rose Bowl

○ ○ ○

I t was probably the biggest play of my career at Ohio State. In fact, it's the most memorable play of my career, either in college or the pros.

Ray Griffin

safety (1974–77),
on his late fourth-quarter, game-altering interception against Michigan in 1975

BUCKS TIE MARK
FOR GREATEST
COMEBACK EVER

After trailing Minnesota, 31–0, Ohio State entered the NCAA record books, tying the mark for the greatest turnaround in major-college football history, as the Buckeyes rallied for an astonishing 41–37 win over the Gophers at the Metrodome, October 28, 1989.

OSU ultimately got on the scoreboard ten seconds before the end of the first half, on a run by tailback Carlos Snow. In the second half, it was nearly all Buckeyes, as quarterback Greg Frey, passing for 362 yards and three touchdowns, engineered the improbable comeback.

Ohio State tallied twice on fourth-down plays and executed three two-point conversions during the hectic run. With just 51 seconds remaining, OSU flankerback Jeff Graham hauled in the winning touchdown pass.

The standard for the greatest collegiate comeback was set by Maryland against Miami (Fla.) in 1984, when the Terps rebounded to beat the Hurricanes, 42–40.

J oe Germaine was like a surgeon going down that field. We got a great mismatch on that last drive. That guy had no chance trying to cover David Boston. He looked like a spastic to be honest with you. It was like shooting fish in a barrel.

John Cooper

on the Buckeyes' game-winning drive that began with just 1:40 remaining in the 1997 Rose Bowl, decided on Germaine's 19-yard toss to Boston with 19 seconds left to give OSU a 17–14 win over second-ranked Arizona State, depriving the Sun Devils of a possible national crown. Germaine was named MVP of the game

Perhaps more than the title game itself, I'll remember the improbable events leading up to that almost surreal night in the desert—the fourth-and-one touchdown pass to Michael Jenkins to beat Purdue; the overtime escape at Illinois the following week; and Will Allen's goal-line interception on the final play against bitter rival Michigan the week after that.

Jon Spencer

on the 2002 regular season

O O O

We called the play at the line of scrimmage. No one was thinking about our season hanging on one play.

Craig Krenzel

quarterback (2000–03),
on the epic fourth-and-one call resulting in
Michael Jenkins's 37-yard game-winning
touchdown pass from Krenzel to beat Purdue,
10–6, with 1:36 remaining for the Buckeyes'
11th consecutive win of 2002

That is the play of the year right now. Looking back, I'm glad we didn't call a timeout, because then maybe we start thinking, *OK, this is it.* We just went out, called the play, and it worked. If you do take a timeout there, you might seize up.

Ben Hartsock

on the thrilling conclusion to the 2002 Purdue game, won by OSU to remain undefeated at 11–0

○ ○ ○

The wind was tough. The one thing Craig does is step up and throw a tight spiral. He threw a bomb. He had good form when he threw it.

Jim Tressel

on quarterback Craig Krenzel's bold fourth-down call that resulted in a game-winning touchdown pass to beat Purdue in 2002, 10–6

After I threw, I got hit. While the ball was in the air, I saw a lot of contact going on in the corner, but after that I was laying on the ground. The ball fell incomplete and Miami rushed the field and I just kind of sat there. It was just a feeling of dejection, thinking that the game was over and knowing how hard we played, how much effort we put in, and thinking that we weren't victorious. I thought there was contact, but I didn't see the flag until after I got up. I think it was the right call, and fortunately, we capitalized on it.

Craig Krenzel

on the controversial fourth-down flag in the second overtime of the 2002 national championship game against Miami, with the Hurricanes leading, 24–17. The late interference call against Miami's Glenn Sharp on Krenzel's end-zone pass to Chris Gamble gave the Buckeyes a second life, with a first down at the Miami 2. Krenzel scored the tying TD, as the Bucks went on to win, 31–24

I got the best jump on that snap that I ever had in my life. It was just me and [Miami quarterback Ken] Dorsey, and I told myself, *Don't miss him . . . just don't miss him.* So many times you see a guy who has a kill shot at the quarterback, and he ends up missing him. I grabbed him and got him to the ground, and I saw that he didn't have the ball, but I didn't know what happened. It wasn't until Coach [Mark] Snyder ran up to me that I realized it was over and we had won the national championship.

Cie Grant

on the final play of the 2002 double-overtime national championship game win over Miami

oming back from the brink with two fourth-down conversions in the first OT, the Buckeyes rode Maurice Clarett's five-yard run and an ensuing goal-line stand to a 31–24 double-overtime victory over the Miami Hurricanes in Sun Devil Stadium. The improbable ending to an improbable OSU season delivered the underrated Buckeyes to their first consensus title since 1968. Ohio State became the first major-college team to complete a 14–0 season.

Jon Spencer

O   O   O

t makes for an ESPN Classic game, but it also makes for lesser years on your life.

Ben Hartsock

*on the nail-biting, double-overtime win
over Miami for the 2002 national crown*

I saw the guy, so I had to make something happen real quick. Once you see a touchdown, there's no need to make a move. You just use your speed.

Ted Ginn Jr.

on his 82-yard third-quarter punt return for a touchdown against Michigan in 2004 that broke open a tight 20–14 game for OSU. Ginn's fourth scoring punt return of the year set new school and Big Ten records, and matched the NCAA mark, in the Buckeyes' 37–21 win

THE OHIO STATE BUCKEYES ALL-TIME TEAM

*T*he selecting of any all-time team without fail is an angst/ecstacy undertaking. Under no circumstances can a Vic Janowicz be left off such an aggregation, so one digs deeper into his glittering dossier. Janowicz, the 1950 Heisman Trophy winner considered by many to be the finest all-around athlete ever to grace the Columbus campus, in addition to his many offensive skills, was also a superb punter, place-kicker, and defensive back, the latter a position he brilliantly manned during the two-way days of his era.

When you have six outstanding backs, five of whom have earned the Heisman, some will, regrettably, be left off an all-time team. In this instance, Les Horvath, the consummate wartime two-way star, and more recently, Eddie George, the big back of the mid-nineties, were forced to sit on the pine, along with OSU's storybook immortal Chic Harley.

Jim Stillwagon's formidable all-star presence dictated a tough makeup on defense. Go with the relentless Outland and Lombardi Trophy winner and you've dictated a 5–2 scheme, leaving out several worthy candidates at linebacker, Tom Cousineau most prominent among them.

But at least one all-time position is immutable: mascot. That longstanding (1965) reveler of OSU football exploits, Brutus Buckeye, rules his gridiron-perimeter turf without peer.

THE BUCKEYES ALL-TIME TEAM

OFFENSE

Wes Fesler, *wide receiver*
Orlando Pace, *tackle*
Jim Parker, *guard*
LeCharles Bentley, *center*
Aurealius Thomas, *guard*
John Hicks, *tackle*
Cris Carter, *wide receiver*
Rex Kern, *quarterback*
Howard Cassady, *halfback*
Bob Ferguson, *fullback*
Archie Griffin, *tailback*

DEFENSE

Jim Houston, *defensive end*
Bill Willis, *defensive tackle*
Jim Stillwagon, *middle guard*
Dan Wilkinson, *defensive tackle*
Mike Vrabel, *defensive end*
Chris Spielman, *linebacker*
Randy Gradishar, *linebacker*
Antoine Winfield, *cornerback*
Vic Janowicz, *free safety*
Mike Doss, *strong safety*
Jack Tatum, *cornerback*

SPECIALISTS

Tom Tupa, *punter*
Mike Nugent, *kicker*
Neal Colzie, *punt returner*
Tom Barrington, *kick returner*

Woody Hayes, *head coach*

WES FESLER

End (1928–30)

All-America (1928, '29, '30),
Chicago Tribune Big Ten MVP (1930),
All-Big Ten (1928, '29, '30),
College Football Hall of Fame (1954)

e was the greatest athlete I've ever seen.

Dick Larkins

tackle/end (1928–30)/
onetime OSU athletic director,
on three-time All-American and later Buckeyes
head coach Wes Fesler, who also starred in
basketball and baseball for Ohio State

ORLANDO PACE

Left Tackle (1994–96)

All-America (1995, '96),
first two-time winner
of the Vince Lombardi Trophy (1995, '96),
Outland Trophy winner (1996),
Football News Offensive Player of the Year (1996),
All-Big Ten (1995, '96),
Chicago Tribune Big Ten MVP (1996)

In my eight seasons at Illinois, he and Tony Mandarich have been the two most dominant offensive linemen we've ever played. It's rare that an offensive lineman can make you change a game plan.

Lou Tepper
on Orlando Pace

JIM PARKER

Guard (1954–56)

All-America (1955, '56),
Outland Trophy winner (1956),
All-Big Ten (1955, '56),
College Football Hall of Fame (1974)

I n those days, we had to keep our hands
in. If Jim could have used his hands the
way they allow you to use them now, he
might have had a pancake every play.

Frank "Moose" Machinsky

*right tackle (1953–55),
on Jim Parker, a selection on the all-time team
of college football's first 100 years*

LeCharles Bentley

Center (1998–2001)

All-America (2001),
Dave Rimington Award winner (2001),
All-Big Ten (2001),
Big Ten Offensive Lineman of the Year (2001)

H e's one of the finest centers I have ever been around. He has a lot of natural talent, but more than that he worked hard every day to get better at the little things. That is a trait that will serve him well throughout the rest of his life.

Jim Bollman
offensive coordinator (2001–),
on Bentley

AUREALIUS THOMAS

Guard (1955–57)

All-America (1957),
All-Big Ten (1957),
College Football Hall of Fame (1989)

Only 202 pounds, Ohio State's Aurealius Thomas played big enough to make the All-America team at guard in 1957. He lacked size but had tremendous technique as a blocker and mobility as a tackler. In his senior year, 1957, he averaged 52 minutes a game in playing time. He was always able to out-maneuver opponents who were bigger.

College Football Hall of Fame

JOHN HICKS

Tackle (1970, 1972–73)

All-America (1972, '73),
Outland Trophy (1973),
Lombardi Trophy (1973),
All-Big Ten (1972, '73),
Heisman Trophy runner-up (1973),
first player ever to start in three Rose Bowls,
College Football Hall of Fame (2001)

You always felt if you went John's way, it was going to be there. We had that much confidence in him, and John had that much confidence in himself. John was one of those guys who'd say, "Hey, bring it my way." Not only would he tell you that, he'd tell the guy across from him that. He'd tell the defensive player before the ball was snapped, "You better get ready, because we're coming at you."

Archie Griffin
on John Hicks

CRIS CARTER

Split End (1984–86)

All-America (1986),
All-Big Ten (1985, '86)

O hio State is a team of big plays and they made them today. Cris Carter made a couple of catches that I thought might be interceptions by us. Instead, he caught them. It might have been a different game had we made those interceptions.

Jackie Sherrill

*former Texas A&M head coach,
on Carter's performance in OSU's 28–12
win over the Aggies in the 1987 Cotton Bowl*

REX KERN

Quarterback (1968–70)

All-America (1969),
1969 Rose Bowl MVP,
Rose Bowl Hall of Fame (1991)

W hen I idolized him as a youngster, I thought he did everything perfect.

Jim Tressel

on Rex Kern

HOWARD "HOPALONG" CASSADY

Halfback (1952–55)

All-America (1954, '55),
Heisman Trophy winner (1955),
Maxwell Award winner (1955),
Associated Press Athlete of the Year (1955),
All-Big Ten (1954, '55),
College Football Hall of Fame (1979)

So brilliant and consistent was Howard Cassady's play throughout the 1955 season that he was the recipient of the coveted Heisman Trophy. Cassady carried the ball 161 times during the nine-game season, netting 958 yards for a remarkable average of 5.9 yards per carry. He rushed for 14 touchdowns and scored another on a punt return. He led the team in rushing, total offense, scoring, punt returns, and kickoff returns. And he played an average of over 53 minutes per game. He even completed two passes on surprise halfback pass plays. Cassady, who weighed only 172 as a senior, was easily the most popular Ohio State football player since Chic Harley.

Marvin Homan
Paul Hornung

Bob Ferguson

Fullback (1959–61)

All-America (1960, '61),
Maxwell Award winner (1961),
All-Big Ten (1960, '61),
College Football Hall of Fame (1996)

Fullback Bob Ferguson playing his last collegiate game, rushed for 152 yards and four touchdowns to become the first Ohio State player to score four TDs in an Ohio State-Michigan game.

Jack Park

*on the Buckeyes' two-time All-American, closing
out his career during OSU's 50–20 demolition
of Michigan in 1961. It was also Ohio State's
400th all-time victory*

ARCHIE GRIFFIN

Tailback (1972–75)

All-America (1973, '74, '75),
Heisman Trophy winner (1974, '75),
Maxwell Award winner (1975),
Walter Camp Award winner (1974, '75),
All-Big Ten (1973, '74, '75),
Chicago Tribune Big Ten MVP (1973, '74),
Rose Bowl Hall of Fame (1990),
only player ever to start in four Rose Bowls,
College Football Hall of Fame (1986)

He's a better young man than he is a football player, and he's the best football player I've ever seen.

Woody Hayes
*on two-time Heisman Trophy winner
Archie Griffin*

O O O

He was the first player since Doak Walker—a quarter of a century earlier—to be named a first-team UPI All-American three straight years.

Alan Natali
on Archie Griffin

JIM HOUSTON

Defensive End (1957–59)

All-America (1958, '59),
All-Big Ten (1958, '59),
College Football Hall of Fame (2005)

The esteemed scout and football historian Esco Sarkkinen always claimed that Jim Houston was the best end he had ever coached. Houston was an All-American for OSU in 1958 and '59, then enjoyed a distinguished 12-year career with the Cleveland Browns.

Todd W. Skipton
author

BILL WILLIS

Defensive Tackle (1942–44)

All-America (1943, '44),
All-Big Ten (1943, '44),
College Football Hall of Fame (1971),
Pro Football Hall of Fame (1977)

Considered one of the all-time great athletes ever to play for Ohio State, Bill Willis has the unique distinction of belonging to the Ohio high school, Ohio State University athletics, college football, and pro football halls of fame. A willowy 6–2 and 215 pounds, he was a devastating blocker on offense and a punishing, relentless tackler on defense, in becoming Ohio State's first African-American All-American.

**Ohio State 2004 Football
Media Guide**

JIM STILLWAGON

Middle Guard (1968–70)

All-America (1969, '70),
Outland Trophy winner (1970),
Lombardi Trophy winner (1970),
All-Big Ten (1969, '70),
College Football Hall of Fame (1991)

I 'll tell you who were the guys who really impressed me . . . Jim Stillwagon and Doug Adams. When I switched over to defense, I used to go over there sometimes, and they were over there killing people. I kind of looked at those two guys and said, "Man, we could have something here."

Jack Tatum

on the Buckeyes' headhunting middle guard and linebacker, respectively, from the 1968 national championship team

DAN WILKINSON

Defensive Tackle (1991–93)

All-America (1993),
All-Big Ten (1992, '93)

The 6–5, 300-pound "Big Daddy" started as a sophomore in 1992 and won All-Big Ten honors. Blessed with an incredible combination of size, strength, and speed, Wilkinson was the dominant defensive lineman in college football as a junior in 1993. No one could block him one-on-one. At season's end, he again won All-Big Ten laurels and was a consensus All-America pick. He was the No. 1 overall pick in the 1994 NFL draft [Cincinnati].

**Ohio State 2004 Football
Media Guide**

MIKE VRABEL
Defensive End (1993–96)
All-America (1995, '96),
All-Big Ten (1994, '95, '96)

V rabel made his mark as one of the most tenacious and feared pass rushers in Ohio State history. He owns every OSU season [13 in 1996] and career [36] sack record. He also finished his career as the Buckeyes' all-time leader in tackles-for-loss [66]. In his junior and senior years, Vrabel was named the Big Ten Conference's Defensive Lineman of the Year.

**Ohio State 2004 Football
Media Guide**

CHRIS SPIELMAN

Linebacker (1984–87)

All-America (1986, '87),
Lombardi Award winner (1987),
All-Big Ten (1985, '86, '87)

During summer practice, we were doing live goal-line hitting, and I was introduced to the difference between high school and college football. As I got the ball and saw the hole open up, I went through it and suddenly I ran into a brick wall. I had never been hit so hard in my entire sports life. The hit was so hard that I still have visions of it in my sleep. Mr. Chris Spielman was on the other end of the hit. His helmet hit smack in the middle of my chest, snot flew from my nose, and the pads came out of my helmet. My shoulder pads came undone, and my shoulder popped out of place. To add insult to my injuries, he spit tobacco right between my eyes. "Welcome to Ohio State football," he said.

Carlos Snow

RANDY GRADISHAR

Linebacker (1971–73)

All-America (1972, '73),
All-Big Ten (1971, '72, '73),
College Football Hall of Fame (1998)

Randy had everything—size [6–3, 236], speed to get outside, toughness to fight through blocks, and an uncanny ability to be at the right place at the right time. Despite wearing a knee brace during the 1972 season, Randy logged 17 tackles against Michigan State and two weeks later 15 against Michigan for two of the greatest defensive feats in Buckeye history But the most familiar sight was big No. 53 roaming from sideline to sideline—wherever the action happened to be.

Paul Hornung

ANTOINE WINFIELD

Cornerback (1995–98)

All-America (1997, '98),
Jim Thorpe Award winner (1998),
All-Big Ten (1997, '98)

We've had some great defensive backs here, guys like Shawn Springs, Ty Howard, and Marlon Kerner. There were some great defensive backs who played here before I came. There are a bunch of them on the wall in there as All-Americans. But [till now] we've never had a Jim Thorpe Award winner. I don't know if we've ever had one as good as Antoine Winfield.

John Cooper

VIC JANOWICZ

Free Safety (1949–51)

All-America (1950),
Heisman Trophy winner (1950),
All-Big Ten (1950, '51),
Chicago Tribune Big Ten MVP (1950),
College Football Hall of Fame (1976)

The great Vic Janowicz is the closest player in Ohio State history to be compared with Chic Harley. . . . Many times an opposing player burst through the middle or skirted the end and thought he was in the clear until he was confronted by Vic, who generally hit an opponent so hard that sometimes I felt sorry for the other player. He was a vicious tackler and when he hit someone they went down in a heap!

Howard E. Wentz
author

MIKE DOSS

Strong Safety (1999–2002)

All-America (2000, '01, '02),
All-Big Ten (2000, '01, '02),
2003 Fiesta Bowl Defensive MVP,
Big Ten Defensive Player of the Year (2002)

Staying at Ohio State for his final season enabled safety Mike Doss to become only the seventh three-time All-American in school history. He was a finalist for the Jim Thorpe Award, given to the nation's top defensive back, was named Big Ten Defensive Player of the Year, and earned Associated Press first-team All-America accolades.

Jon Spencer

JACK TATUM

Cornerback (1968–70)

All-America (1969, '70),
All-Big Ten (1968, '69, '70),
College Football Hall of Fame (2004)

I never thought anyone could cover me man-for-man before, but Jack Tatum sure did today.

Leroy Keyes

*Purdue consensus All-America halfback (1968),
on the OSU All-America cornerback. Tatum
personally shut down the vaunted Keyes,
holding him to just 19 yards in seven carries
and only 44 yards on four receptions,
in the critical 13–0 Buckeye win
over the Boilermakers in Ohio State's
national championship season of 1968*

TOM TUPA

Punter (1984–87)

All-America (1987),
All-Big Ten (1984, '85, '87)

You'll get a fight from Skladany supporters here, and possibly from Andy Groom's camp, but Tupa's splendid career average at OSU—44.7—is a full two yards longer than Skladany's cumulative mark. Though Groom's 45.0 beats Tupa by 0.3 yards, Tupa booted twice as many punts as Groom [214 to 109] over the course of his Buckeye career. Tupa also earned Associated Press first-team All-America recognition, the nation's most prestigious A-A aggregate, something the three-time All-American Skladany failed to achieve.

MIKE NUGENT

Kicker (2001–04)

All-America (2002, 2004),
Lou Groza Award winner (2004)

He's like a Tiger Woods: a concise, precise swing, very fluid, not a lot of movement to it, and not all over the place. He's very athletic and has very few moving parts. He's the guy I want.

Mike Westhoff

*New York Jets special-teams coach,
on Lou Groza Award winner Nugent, who set
19 records while at Ohio State. Westhoff got his
wish, when the Jets took Nugent with the
26th pick in the 2005 NFL draft*

NEAL COLZIE
Punt Returner (1972–74)
All-America (1974),
All-Big Ten (1973, '74)

H e's the best punt returner I've ever seen.

Woody Hayes
on Neal Colzie

TOM BARRINGTON
Kick Returner (1963–65)

W *hile it's true that both Maurice Hall [1,642] and Ken-Yon Rambo [1,410] both recorded twice the number of yards in kick-off returns than Barrington registered [730], it is Barrington's 30.4-yard career average return and 34.3 average return in 1965 that are still Ohio State standards.*

WOODY HAYES

Head Coach (1951–78)

National championships (3),
Big Ten championships (13),
Rose Bowl victories (4),
Rose Bowl Hall of Fame (1989),
College Football Hall of Fame (1983)

God is not dead. He is alive and coaching at Ohio State.

**Banner waved during the
1968 Michigan game**

in reference to Woody Hayes

THE GREAT BUCKEYE TEAMS

T here is nothing individual about any national championship—not the one the 1968 Buckeyes won, nor the one that the 2002 team claimed. Individuals don't win championships. Teams do.

Rex Kern

In 1917, Coach John Wilce's powerful Buckeye football machine, paced by the gifted Chic Harley, did not give up a single touchdown all season, yielding only field goals to Indiana and Wisconsin.

Marvin Homan
Paul Hornung

○ ○ ○

For a coach so geared to and immersed in offense, Francis Schmidt's teams had remarkable defensive statistics, yielding 34, 57, 27, and 23 points in his first four seasons, while the Buckeyes scored 267, 237, 160, and 125. Maybe of even greater import, he won four straight over Michigan, all by shutouts and by a margin of 114 total points.

Marvin Homan
Paul Hornung
on Schmidt's Buckeye teams of 1934–40

T he Associated Press named Ohio State the best team in the nation [in 1942]. Only the announcement of peace could have had a more joyous effect on Columbus, Ohio.

J. Timothy Weigel

O   O   O

T he 1944 Buckeyes produced the first unbeaten-untied record [9–0] since 1916; a Big Ten championship [5–0]; the unofficial "civilian national championship" [Army was No. 1 in the AP poll]; boasted the year's Heisman Trophy winner and Big Ten MVP in Les Horvath; and had more All-Americans [four] than in any previous year.

**Marvin Homan
Paul Hornung**

O   O   O

T he heart-stopping 1949 Buckeyes were a come-from-behind team that did it often enough to get to Pasadena for the first time since 1921.

J. Timothy Weigel

The 1954 Ohio State University football team could be slightly improved over last year's squad, but there is considerable doubt whether the six-won, three-lost record of the '53 team can be bettered.

OSU press book for 1954

FAST FACT: The Buckeyes proved their own publicity mill wrong, going on to become national champs in '54.

O   O   O

Woody Hayes's 1954 squad became the first Big Ten team to win seven conference games in one season since Amos Alonzo Stagg's Chicago Maroons won seven in 1913, the year Hayes was born.

Jack Park

That Buckeye team might have been as fine a squad as any Woody Hayes had ever coached—including the '54 and '68 national champion teams.

J. Timothy Weigel
on the 1961 team

O O O

Twelve sophomores worked themselves into the starting rotation that season. That class eventually produced six All-Americans, nine all-Big Ten players, and 13 NFL draft picks.

Jay Hansen
sportswriter,
Newspaper Network of Central Ohio,
on the sophomore-dominated lineup of the
1968 national championship team

O O O

The important thing was we didn't know we were making history at the time. We just went game by game, tried to correct our mistakes, and build on what we learned.

Rex Kern
on the '68 Bucks

The sophomores came in and raised the bar a bit. They walked to the beat of a different drummer. They went out and had a lot of fun so we went out and had a lot of fun. They had great attitudes, and they all expected to play and win.

Jim Otis

on the Super Sophs of '68

○   ○   ○

The 1967 group was perhaps the best college team ever recruited.

Woody Hayes

FAST FACT: Of that extraordinary recruiting class, four were future first-round NFL draft choices and six made All-America (two of them twice), as Ohio State went 27–2 over the period from 1968 through 1970, winning a national championship and two outright Big Ten crowns.

You're the best team I ever played against!

O.J. Simpson
USC's Heisman Trophy-winning running back, to the 1968 Ohio State Buckeyes in their locker room following OSU's Rose Bowl victory over Simpson and the Trojans, 27–16

○ ○ ○

The whole thing was a meld of unusual, really talented football players.

Esco Sarkkinen
on the 1968 national champion Buckeyes

○ ○ ○

We had great chemistry on the team. The sophomores were really talented, but the upperclassmen maintained leadership of the team.

Lou Holtz
on the '68 Buckeyes

○ ○ ○

I don't know what the magic was. It was an intangible relationship between the team and Woody.

Larry Zelina
*wingback (1968–70),
on the 1968 team*

The thing I remember most about that year [1968] was that we were having success but it was probably the most fun I ever had playing football. It was because of the group of guys we were with. That one year, our sophomore year. It was unexpected, we were naïve and young. We had a ball.

Jack Tatum

O O O

That's probably the finest football team there's ever been.

Fred A. Taylor
TCU head coach,
after experiencing a 62–0 defeat
at the hands of the Buckeyes
in the 1969 season opener

The 1969 Buckeyes were probably the best team we ever put together, probably the best team that ever played college football. That team would have been national champions without a doubt. But Bo beat us!

Woody Hayes
*on the historic 24–12 defeat by Michigan
in Ann Arbor to close out the 1969 season,
ending top-ranked Ohio State's certain
national championship season*

○ ○ ○

For my money, that's the finest team ever put together in college football history. That group could finish respectably in the NFL right now, they have so much talent and depth.

John Coatta
*Wisconsin head coach (1967–69),
after the Buckeyes drilled the Badgers, 62–7,
late in the 1969 season*

H ey! We just beat the team of the century!

Jim Plunkett
*Stanford 1970 consensus All-America
quarterback and college football Hall of Famer,
after leading the Cardinal to a 27–17 upset of
top-ranked OSU in the 1971 Rose Bowl*

O   O   O

W e were a great team. But we could
have been greater.

John Brockington
*on the 1968–70 Buckeyes, who are
occasionally remembered more for their two
losses in three seasons (27–2 overall) than for
their many achievements, including three
Big Ten titles and a national crown*

O   O   O

I s this the best single class we ever had
here? Hell, they are the best class anybody ever had!

Woody Hayes
on his class of 1970

T heir offense is as great as I've ever seen.

Bob Blackmon

on the 1974 Ohio State Buckeyes that featured
tailback Archie Griffin, fullbacks Pete Johnson
and Champ Henson, quarterback Cornelius
Greene, and wingback Brian Baschnagel

O   O   O

G riffin and his fellow seniors did leave with one remarkable distinction: They never lost a game in Ohio Stadium in their four varsity years [1972–75].

Marvin Homan
Paul Hornung

O   O   O

T hey're no longer three yards and a cloud of dust. Now they're 12 yards and a mass of humanity.

Cal Stoll

former head coach, University of Minnesota,
on the 1973 Buckeyes

That '75 team . . . now we had a team there. We were picked to finish about third in the Big Ten heading into that season. . . . In those four years, I am proud to say that we never lost to Michigan.

Archie Griffin

○ ○ ○

In my playing days, Woody Hayes was a stickler for detail. Jim Tressel said the 2002 team was going back to the basics; these Buckeyes were going to learn from the ground up, much like Woody's Ohio State teams did. I firmly believe a national championship was hatched that day.

Rex Kern

Before the game, Coach Tressel told us, "Seize this opportunity. If you are a junior, sophomore or a freshman, don't think you'll ever get here again and have another chance. This is it! Seize it! It has been 34 years since Ohio State last won a national championship. Know that you are playing for all of Ohio State's fans, alumni, and former players. Now go do it!"

Cie Grant

O O O

One quality that all undefeated teams share is a certain resourcefulness, an ability to dance through dangerous situations. Ohio State's record was flawless not because it obliterated every opponent—although it did that to more than a few—but because it kept its feet when staggered.

Phil Taylor

Sports Illustrated,
on the 2002 Bucks

If the Buckeyes were lucky enough to survive those end zone calls against Illinois, they were also resilient enough to shake off the Illini's tying field goal as regulation time expired. Down 6–3 to Purdue and 9–7 to hated Michigan, Ohio State rallied for the winning touchdown in the fourth quarter both times. That kind of poise is what undefeated seasons require.

Phil Taylor
on the 2002 team

O O O

It's been my belief that the tradition and honor at Ohio State has long been set before me and will be long set after me. Watching the guys win the [2002] national championship confirmed that belief.

Chris Spielman

FIELDS
OF PLAY

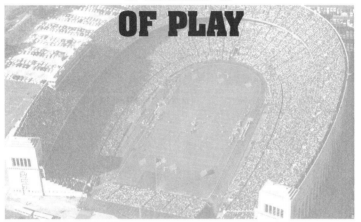

The bigness of it, that monster building, the Horseshoe. God, when we went in and looked down on that field, it was just so pretty and everything: Players in colored uniforms and a green field with white stripes. Really big and really pretty. Listenin' to it on the radio and imaginin' and then comin' in and seein' it like that is just two different things.

Don Hurley
Buckeye fan

After the 1897 season, the North Athletic Field grounds, west of Neil Avenue and north of the North Dormitory, were relocated to land along High Street extending north to what is now Woodruff Avenue. The new football field ran parallel to High Street and the grandstand was moved from its former site and placed on the west side of the football field. The new area was called "University Field," renamed "Ohio Field" in 1908.

Marvin Homan
Paul Hornung

O O O

There was great anticipation and excitement when the Buckeyes opened the 1922 season in the new [Ohio] Stadium, on October 7, against Ohio Wesleyan. Ohio State won, 5–0, before a crowd of 25,000.

Marvin Homan
Paul Hornung

Ohio Stadium

The Buckeye faithful were invited to come out and dig up patches for enshrinement around Ohio. Woody blessed each out-going chunk of sod like the French bless the bones at Verdun.

J. Timothy Weigel

on the transition at Ohio Stadium from natural grass to artificial turf in 1971

○ ○ ○

Woody's wife, Anne, took a wheelbarrow full home to distribute patches up and down the block and then placed a hunk in Hayes's front yard. One sweet old lady showed up at the affair and measured a six-by-three-foot patch which she said would be placed on her husband's grave.

J. Timothy Weigel

on the above-mentioned Ohio Stadium sod dispersed to Buckeye fans before artificial turf was laid down in '71

T he Ohio Stadium press box was so cold that the copying machine wouldn't work, and the staff had no way of providing game statistics for the sportswriters. Finally, a resourceful individual poured vodka into the machine's gears. The 'lubricant' got it going, and the machine hummed along reasonably well the remainder of the afternoon.

Roger Stanton
former publisher of Football News,
*on the arctic-like conditions of the 1964
Michigan-OSU game*

O   O   O

T il I die, I'll still feel that feelin' that it's great to walk into that tremendous stadium they got up there. The memories, the tradition behind it, the football greats, and everything. I just like to go in there.

Don Hurley

So well constructed was Ohio Stadium that it remains sound, solid, and safe after 68 years of use, while many other athletic facilities, much newer and considerably more costly, have been either substantially reinforced or even abandoned as unsafe.

Marvin Homan
Paul Hornung
1990

O   O   O

All the stories I'd heard about running out of that tunnel before a game for the first time were true. That is a highlight of "the shoe" for everyone who has ever played there. Still today, after all these years, it remains my ultimate feeling.

Pepper Johnson

I had seen the team come out of that tunnel a dozen times . . . with coach Bruce standing in front and the police holding the team back. I just didn't know what it would be like to run onto that field. Literally, my feet didn't touch the ground that first time in my freshman season. It was so exciting. You wind up chasing that feeling again for the rest of your life.

Cris Carter
wide receiver (1984–86)/All-America (1986)

The Horseshoe. Like visiting an old friend. I've seen it empty and staid. I've seen it as a powder keg of emotion for an entire community. I've howled in it, frozen in it, let loose all feelings of joy in the stands, and pumped my fist under the table in the press box. I've also felt sick to my stomach in it, seen seasons of greatness sour in one blink of the eye. I still marvel at the majesty of the stadium and how it pulls me into focus whether as a frenetic, jam-packed setting on game day or as an awe-inspiring, world-class edifice. I'm not ashamed to say I've walked into the stadium and had my eyes mist up. I'm not ashamed to say it because I know many others have experienced the same thing.

Jeff Rapp
author

RIVALRIES: THAT TEAM UP NORTH

C hic Harley, in almost magical style, intercepted four of Michigan's 18 passes to erase any further threats.

Jack Park

on the Buckeye immortal's contributions to Ohio State's first-ever victory over Michigan, a 13–3 win at Ann Arbor's old Ferry Field in 1919. Both teams had entered the fray undefeated and unscored upon. In addition to his marvelous defensive work, Harley also scored the game's final TD on a 42-yard run and punted 11 times for a 42-yard average.

FAST FACT: *Michigan had won 13 and tied two in the first 15 meetings between the two teams.*

Without doubt, the 1926 game with Michigan ranks as one of the most thrilling and most memorable in the long history of Ohio Stadium. The game had everything, trick plays, long runs, hard hitting defensive play and, unfortunately, fumbles, for Ohio State lost the game trying to field a bouncing punt deep in Ohio territory only to fumble. Michigan recovered and scored, winning the game, 17–16, thus dashing Ohio State's undefeated season and championship hopes.

Marvin Homan
Paul Hornung

FAST FACT: *Legendary Michigan quarterback and 2005 Pro Football Hall of Fame inductee Benny Friedman captained the Wolverines in that epic match, which also featured OSU All-America fullback Marty Karow, who later coached Buckeye baseball teams for a quarter of a century.*

The most stirring tie with which I've ever been associated.

Paul Brown

on the 1941 Ohio State-Michigan season finale at Ann Arbor that ended in a 20–20 tie. As the teams lined up for the decisive extra point, after Michigan had pulled even with a late touchdown drive, Paul Brown called timeout— then another. When Brown and his charges could stall no longer, Michigan kicked—and missed! Brown would later insist that he called the timeouts not as a strategy but because he couldn't bear to see his team lose after having waged such a gallant battle

The 1944 game became a permanent part of Rivalry lore.

Greg Emmanuel

FAST FACT: Les Horvath, Ohio State's first Heisman Trophy winner, in 1944, punted and ran the Buckeyes to a see-saw thrilling 18–14 victory. Both schools entered the game looking to win the conference championship. Horvath was involved in a controversial play, fumbling as he went over the Wolverines goal line, but the officials ruled it a touchdown.

○ ○ ○

We'll coast and push this goddam car to the Ohio line before I give this state a nickel of my money!

Woody Hayes

running on empty on a recruiting trip into Michigan with assistant coach Ed Ferkany, circa 1972–73

FAST FACT: The above tale is reportedly true. One version claims that Hayes indeed did run out of gas and pushed the car seven miles to the state line.

WOLVERINES LOSE THEIR COOL ON STRANGE PLAY

Michigan had something to kick about after the 1955 battle with archrival Ohio State.

With the Buckeyes having taken an 11–0 lead in the fourth quarter at Ann Arbor following a safety against the Wolverines, Michigan All-American Ron Kramer attempted an onside kick. But in a rare miscue, the big end completely missed the ball.

Officials gave possession to Ohio State at the Michigan 20, and the Wolverines lost their cool. Tempers raged and Michigan was penalized for a personal foul.

Another penalty placed the ball on the Michigan 1, from where OSU fullback Don Vicic scored to push the Bucks ahead, 17–0.

The strange play helped secure Ohio State's second consecutive outright Big Ten title.

T hose two points might mean more to us than they would for them.

Woody Hayes

defending his decision to go for a two-point conversion leading archrival Michigan 48–20 on the final play of the 1961 game. Immediately prior to the successful two-point conversion, Hayes had inserted passer Joe Sparma into the lineup and instructed him to pass. Sparma responded with a 37-yard scoring aerial with three seconds remaining, incensing Michigan fans

FAST FACT: *Hayes's offense amassed 512 yards in the 30-point victory, Ohio State's 400th.*

O   O   O

N o other regularly scheduled game between any two teams in any sport is as consequential, as often.

Greg Emmanuel

on the Ohio State-Michigan rivalry

The way we dominated them in the second half was the greatest feeling in my athletic career.

Dave Foley

tackle (1966–68),
on the 1968 Michigan game. With a Rose Bowl
berth, an outright Big Ten title, and their first
undefeated season since 1944 on the line,
the Buckeyes ground out 421 yards rushing and
notched 24 first downs, while fullback Jim Otis
tied Bob Ferguson's school record of four
touchdowns in a single game, en route to a
50–14 crushing of the Wolverines

B ecause I couldn't go for three.

Woody Hayes

*his outrageous response to the question of why
the Buckeyes went for two points after scoring
their final touchdown, giving them a 36-point
lead in a 50–14 rout of the Wolverines in
1968, an unforgivable affront to Michigan fans*

O   O   O

A ll good things must come to an end,
and that's what happened today. We
just got outplayed, outpunched, and out-
coached.

Woody Hayes

*after the devastating 24–12 loss to Michigan in
1969, when the Buckeyes were undefeated and
ranked No. 1 in the country*

I t'll Be A L-O-N-G Winter

***Columbus Dispatch* headline**
Nov. 23, 1969,
predicting the regional emotional climate
in the woeful wake of the 24–12 loss
to Michigan, during which the Buckeyes had
six passes intercepted, killing top-ranked OSU's
bid for a second successive national title

O   O   O

W e won't alibi or apologize for the last defeat any more than for the previous 22 wins.

Woody Hayes
to an Appreciation Banquet audience
after the deflating loss to Michigan closed out
the 1969 season for the national
championship-bound Buckeyes

Woody would get you ready for Michigan all year. We used to say that Michigan was a separate season in itself. Spring practice we'd be getting ready for Michigan's defense. It was a constant preparation for that game—the whole season every Monday.

Archie Griffin

O O O

Coming into the 1970 Game, both teams were undefeated and untied for the first time in the history of the series. Ohio State ranked number 1, and Michigan was right behind at number 2. Michigan's Lance Scheffer fumbled the opening kick-off, and the Wolverines never regained their poise. The first battle between undefeated titans ended 20–9, and Hayes had his revenge.

Greg Emmanuel

FAST FACT: Many regard the 1969 loss to Michigan as the worst defeat in Buckeye annals. Hayes seethed for an entire year following the 24–12 Wolverine victory, and his obsession carried over to the team. "I've been thinking about Michigan every morning when I get up for a whole year," admitted quarterback Rex Kern between the 1969 and '70 games.

Woody and Bo were fierce competitors. Instead of Bo going for a field goal, he was going to try for a touchdown, and our defense was going to be there to stop them. But that's what made the thing so exciting.

Archie Griffin

on the 1972 classic: a 14–11 Ohio State victory, sealed when Michigan's Schembechler elected to go for a touchdown on fourth-and-inches instead of kicking a tying field goal

FAST FACT: *The decision illustrates the ferocity of competition between Hayes and Schembechler. A tie, which would have given the Wolverines a share of the Big Ten title and a trip to the Rose Bowl, was eschewed by Schembechler because he wouldn't have beaten Hayes.*

○ ○ ○

This is not a game, this is war.

Woody Hayes

of the OSU-UM rivalry

○ ○ ○

If that was war, sign me up forever.

Bo Schembechler

on the 10-year period, from 1969 through 1978, that he and OSU's Hayes squared off

T he Hayes-Schembechler duels at times almost overshadowed what Woody hailed as "the greatest rivalry in football": Ohio State vs. Michigan. For six straight years, 1972 through 1977, they played for the league title and Rose Bowl invitation. Five resulted in co-championships, the Buckeyes gaining the other outright. Ohio State grabbed the Rose Bowl ring four straight times, Michigan twice. Box score for the 10-year "war": Woody 4, Bo, 5, 1 tie.

Marvin Homan
Paul Hornung

FAST FACT: Hayes and Schembechler faced each other during the decade 1969–78.

After the game, several players hoisted Bruce on their shoulders and marched him around the field. It was the most bittersweet victory in the history of the epic Rivalry.

Greg Emmanuel

on head coach Earle Bruce's final game for Ohio State after being fired from his post earlier in the week of the 1987 Michigan game. OSU sent Bruce off with a 23–20 victory at Ann Arbor

O O O

It's a big game. It's a one-game season. All that stuff is true. Both teams play differently than they play all year.

Greg Bellisari

linebacker (1993–96), on the Michigan-Ohio State rivalry

People come up to me all the time and say, 'So, Coach, are we going to beat Michigan this year?' Now what kind of stupid question is that? No one wants to beat Michigan more than I do. But if you're going to coach football at Ohio State, it's something you have to accept. Michigan means everything to people in Columbus. That's the way it's always been.

John Cooper

FAST FACT: Cooper's impressive 111–43–4 overall record in Columbus was not enough to offset his woeful 2–10–1 mark against Michigan. He was fired after the 2000 season.

This rivalry is like none other. When you go back to Ohio State, and you talk to all the other players from the other years, it's always, "How many times did you beat Michigan? How many pairs of gold pants do you have?" I'm lucky enough to have one. That's what we're judged on.

Scott Terna

punter (1993–94)

O O O

From 1919 to '33, the Ohio State-Illinois contest was the last game of the regular season for both teams. Ohio State and Michigan began the tradition of meeting in the season's final game in '35.

Jack Park

ichigan truly was THE GAME. It was never out of Woody's thoughts—or ours—for good reason. It was a different era back then, a time of risky one-year contracts. We all understood that if we lost three straight games to the Wolverines, Coach Hayes and the rest of us would be out looking for work. If you don't believe me, look at the three years prior to Woody's dismissal.

Esco Sarkkinen

FAST FACT: Hayes's Buckeyes lost to No. 4-, 5-, and 6-ranked Michigan from 1976 through 1978, the only three-year stretch in Hayes's illustrious 28-year-coaching career at OSU that he lost three games in succession to the Wolverines.

If Ohio State had notched a reputation as a graveyard for coaches, it was largely because those coaches consistently failed to whip the Wolverines. During the 20 years prior to Woody Hayes's appointment, only Francis Schmidt had a winning record against Michigan.

J. Timothy Weigel

○ ○ ○

In a game like the Michigan game, if you're not ready to play, you shouldn't be on the field. I think the coaches had to be careful to make sure that we weren't ready to play too soon.

Larry Zelina

We don't give a damn for the whole state of Michigan!

Anonymous Ohio State fan

FAST FACT: The line that blossomed into a legendary Buckeye fight song originated sometime in the 1920s, when Columbus Dispatch *columnist Johnny Jones heard an OSU fan shouting the line in the lobby of the old Deshler-Wallick Hotel in downtown Columbus before a Michigan-Ohio State game. Sung to the tune of "The Old Gray Mare."*

O O O

When you win the championship, you don't have to apologize. You don't have to hang your head. Are we disappointed? You're damned right we are.

Lloyd Carr
*Michigan head coach,
on winning a trip to the 2005 Rose Bowl
after losing to Ohio State, 37–21, in the
2004 regular-season finale*

FAST FACT: This marked only the third time that the loser of the Michigan-Ohio State game had gone to the Rose Bowl. Michigan did it in 1982, and Ohio State in 1996.

O O O

We always hope we'll play our best game against Michigan.

Jim Tressel

THE BUCKEYE FAITHFUL

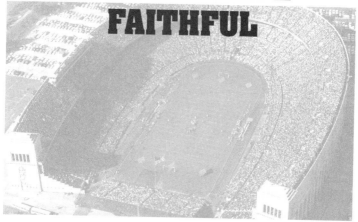

Even if I didn't go to Ohio State, I'd still be an Ohio State fan. It's Ohio State football, then golf, then women. And God is up there, too.

Ohio State supporter

With a great deal of brashness and some very realistic costumes and props, Jerry Marlow, a pharmacist from New Philadelphia, Ohio, has talked his way through the Ohio Stadium gates dressed as an OSU cheerleader, an ABC television camera operator, a game referee, an OSU band director, and a nun. One year, he sat in a section designated for former Buckeye players by impersonating Tad Weed, Ohio State's placekicker in the early 1950s.

Jack Park

FAST FACT: Marlow, a believer in fairness, mails a check for an amount that exceeds the price of a game ticket to Ohio State after each "freebie."

Being a casual Buckeye fan is as feasible as being a half-virgin. You can live in Ann Arbor and not be a Wolverine fan; in Columbus, you're more likely to spot a rhino on the State House steps than a non-Buckeye fan.

Greg Emmanuel

O   O   O

Fans love you today, but they may hate you tomorrow. I'll take what I did with a grain of salt, go back to practice, and try to do the best I can.

Maurice Clarett

tailback (2002),
after his collegiate debut in the season-opening
win over Texas Tech in 2002, in which the
freshman tailback rushed for 175 yards and
three touchdowns

The opening game, probably the biggest thrill of my life, was running out there and hearing that crowd. That crowd! That thing alone was just awesome, and it's also something that was never recreated.

Mike Sensibaugh

safety (1968–70), All-America (1970),
on running out onto the field at Ohio Stadium
for his debut game as a Buckeye, Sept. 28,
1968, against Southern Methodist University

There was a lot of times I didn't think he called the right plays. I raised hell with Woody a few times. I said, "Daggonnit, Woody, you got the player out there too late and cost us a five-yard penalty"; or, "Woody, you called the wrong play." All of us fans give 'im hell, but, you know, we was talkin' to a TV. We wasn't talkin' to his face. You can give a TV a lotta hell.

Don Hurley

fan

◯ ◯ ◯

As far as the people of Columbus are concerned, the OSU Buckeyes are their Yankees, their Green Bay Packers, and their Lakers rolled up into one scarlet-and-gray package.

Greg Emmanuel

This town's totally Buckeye. Every hotel that I've gone to, Ohio State has taken over.

Dr. Chuck Cook

Lancaster, Ohio, fan,
on the city of Phoenix, Arizona, prior to
the 2002 Fiesta Bowl

O O O

It feels more like Columbus than it does Tempe here.

Kathy Motycka

Van Wert, Ohio, fan,
before the 2002 national championship game
in Tempe, Arizona

O O O

Columbus is a drinking town with a football problem.

Seen on a Columbus T-shirt

I remembered Woody talking about these 86,000 screaming people. The first game came around, I went out without my shoulder pads on and looked around. I had more people at my high school games. *Everybody should be here now*, I thought. I've been lied to, and I don't forget a lie. Right away, I'm feeling down. I'm ready to leave. So we go in and put our shoulder pads on, and I'll never forget when they opened that door, and the roar of the crowd hit me like someone took an electric socket and stuck it to me. It was a scary feeling. Right there, you look at all those people, and they look like a disturbed ant bed.

Pete Johnson

The psychological wave is turning in our favor. Keep this crowd hilarious!

Dr. John Wilce

*head coach (1913–28),
imploring the Buckeye cheerleaders
in a game during his OSU tenure*

THE LOCKER ROOM

I don't know if they'll get "it" until more time passes. It will be something very, very special. I hope what they get from it is what it takes to be a champion—all the people that are important, all the things that have to be done, all the lessons learned. If they get that, I don't care if they ever get what it means to be a national champion. I hope they get the lessons.

Jim Tressel

after the monumental 2002 Fiesta Bowl
31–24 double-overtime victory over Miami
for the national championship

The best quarterback in the Big Ten, yet he never took a snap from center or threw a single pass.

Woody Hayes

on OSU basketball legend John Havlicek,
a former high school all-star quarterback
whom Hayes had tried to recruit.
Throughout Havlicek's successful career with
the Buckeye cagers, Hayes always left the
door open for Havlicek's gridiron participation.
After once observing "Hondo" tossing a football
with OSU quarterback Tom Matte,
news reporters noted Havlicek's ability
to throw the ball 70 yards

Everyone seems focused on the potential distraction Maurice Clarett has caused his team with his emotional outbursts. His rants have ranged from complaining that "football is more important than life" at Ohio State to calling school officials "liars" in the way they handled his situation.

Jon Spencer

on the "other" side of Clarett that began to surface toward the close of the 2002 season, drawing national headlines. Clarett's unfortunate saga would continue, ultimately involving litigation and causing the talented tailback eventually to withdraw from Ohio State, having played just that lone 2002 season in scarlet and gray

I remember that John Hicks and I were chosen to be on the *Playboy* All-America team, and the honor meant a visit to the Playboy Mansion, but that magazine was not on Woody's reading list. He didn't believe it would be the right kind of exposure and it wouldn't do Ohio State, John, or me any good, so he wouldn't let us go. With no pictures of us, *Playboy* cut and pasted our heads onto pictures for that article.

Randy Gradishar

THE MIGHTY MOJO OF BOB FERGUSON'S CHINSTRAP

Bob Ferguson and Jim Otis were two of the Buckeyes' finest fullbacks. Ferguson a two-time All-American in, 1960 and '61, finished a close second to Ernie Davis in the Heisman Trophy balloting his senior year. Otis was an All-American in 1969, and his career rushing total of 2,542 yards is the highest of any fullback in Ohio State history.

In his last collegiate game, Ferguson scored four touchdowns while leading the Buckeyes to a 50–20 blasting of Michigan at Ann Arbor. On his way to the dressing room after the game, Ferguson gave his chinstrap to a young Ohio State fan as a souvenir.

Seven years later, in 1968, Ohio State was preparing for its game with Michigan, which would determine the outright Big Ten champion. Both teams entered the contest with 6–0 league records.

At a huge pep rally on campus the Friday evening prior to the big game, the fan to whom Ferguson had given his chinstrap—a person Otis thinks was named Scooter—approached Otis, told him the history of the chinstrap, and gave it to him.

"I showed Ernie Biggs [the trainer] and told him that Bob Ferguson was supposed to have worn this chinstrap against Michigan when he scored four touchdowns," said Otis in the book Ohio State '68: All the Way to the Top. "So we taped it to the inside of my helmet because it didn't have a snap on it.

The next afternoon, like something bordering on the fantastic that could have been scripted in Hollywood, Otis scored four touchdowns and Ohio State again scored 50 points, defeating the Wolverines 50–14. Otis still treasures that famous chinstrap—the one that crossed the Michigan goal line eight times.

From Jack Park and Jim Otis accounts

People ask me, What do you remember about your years at Ohio State playing football? I say, frankly, the only thing I remember are the two freaking losses.

Phil Strickland

guard (1968–70),
referring to the two blemishes on his
and the Class of 1970's near-spotless
27–2 overall record

○ ○ ○

I came back to play with these guys I came in with, had blood, sweat, and tears with. We always said that when it was our turn, we were going to do this. We always had faith we'd have a chance to play for the national championship.

Mike Doss

safety (1999–2002),
who returned to Columbus for his senior year
and helped the Buckeyes to the national title
in 2002

I t's gratifying to be remembered by people. It's an affirmation that you did something special. It's amazing to me that this town still remembers. I can walk into Bob Evans and have breakfast and see pictures of me and Woody and Jack Nicklaus. I think about it, and I get emotional. I'm part of Ohio State history. That's mind-boggling.

Rex Kern

O O O

I n the locker room, Coach Hayes always told us that the finest people we would meet would be in this room. He was right. Those teammates I had on those teams are the greatest people I have ever met. We were not a team just on the football field. We became a team for life.

John Hicks

OHIO STATE NATIONAL CHAMPION ROSTERS

*I*n the five seasons that have yielded national championship teams in Columbus, many a Buckeye has played the cog in the wheel. The following roster listings carry a salute to all the players that have helped spell out "Script Championship" for Ohio State.

1942

9–1

(National champions in Associated Press poll)
Paul Brown, head coach

	Pos.	Ht.	Wt.	Yr.
Appleby, Gordon	C	181	5–11	So
Amling, Martin	G	180	5–9	So
Antennucci, Thomas	E	178	5–11	So
Cleary, Thomas	HB	188	5–11	So
Coleman, Kenneth	C	185	6–1	Jr
Csuri, Charles	**T**	**195**	**6–0**	**Jr**
Dean, Hal	**G**	**190**	**6–0**	**Jr**
Drake, Phillip	QB	185	6–0	So
Dugger, Jack	T	205	6–4	So
Durtschi, William	HB	172	5–8	Jr
Eichwald, Kenneth	E	181	6–4	So
Fekete, Gene	**FB**	**192**	**6–1**	**So**
Frye, Robert	HB	161	5–10	Jr
Hackett, William	G	185	5–9	So
Horvath, Leslie	**HB**	**160**	**5–11**	**Sr**
Houston, Lindel	**G**	**198**	**5–11**	**Jr**
Jabbusch, Robert	G	187	5–10	So
James, Thomas	HB	155	5–9	So
Lipaj, Cyril	FB	180	5–10	So
Lavelli, Dante	E	185	6–1	So
Lynn, George (Captain)	**QB**	**195**	**6–0**	**Jr**
McCafferty, Don	T	202	6–4	Sr
McCormick, Bob	T	198	5–10	Jr
MacDonald, W.	G	182	5–10	So
Matus, Paul	E	178	5–11	So
Naples, Carmen	G	185	5–11	Jr
Palmer, Richard	FB	192	5–10	Jr
Priday, Paul	QB	180	5–10	So
Rees, James	T	199	6–0	So
Roe, Jack	C	180	5–11	Jr
Sarringhaus, Paul	**HB**	**190**	**5–10**	**Jr**
Schneider, Wib	G	175	5–8	Jr
Sedor, William	E	188	6–2	Jr
Selby, Paul	QB	198	5–10	So
Shaw, Robert	**E**	**199**	**6–3**	**Jr**
Slusser, George	HB	170	5–11	So
Souders, Cecil	E	189	6–0	So
Staker, Loren	HB	160	5–11	Sr
Steinberg, Don	**E**	**190**	**6–0**	**Jr**
Vickroy, William	**C**	**190**	**6–0**	**Sr**
Willis, William	**T**	**202**	**6–2**	**So**
White, John	E	190	6–3	So
Taylor, Tom	T	195	6–1	So

Starters in bold

1954
10–0
(Includes 20–7 Rose Bowl victory over Southern California. National champions in Associated Press poll)
Woody Hayes, head coach

	Pos.	Ht.	Wt.	Yr.
Archer, Jack	LH	177	5–10	So
Augenstein, Jack	FB	188	5–10	Jr
Bond, Robert	C	186	5–11	Jr
Borton, John (co-captain)	QB	200	6–1	Sr
Blazeff, Lalo	RE	187	6–0	So
Bobo, Hubert	**FB**	**192**	**6–0**	**So**
Booth, William	QB	178	6–0	Jr
Brubaker, Richard (co-captain)	**RE**	**198**	**6–0**	**Sr**
Campbell, Jack	LE	204	6–2	Jr
Cassady, Howard	**LH**	**177**	**5–10**	**Jr**
Cole, Robert	LG	200	5–10	So
Collmar, William	RE	170	6–1	Jr
Cummings, William	LT	247	6–2	So
Dillman, Thomas	C	192	6–2	So
Dugger, Dean	**LE**	**206**	**6–2**	**Sr**
Ebinger, Elbert	RT	238	6–3	Jr
Ellwood, Frank	LE	192	5–11	So
Guy, Richard	LT	206	6–3	So
Harkrader, Jerry	LH	176	5–9	Jr
Hilinski, Richard	**LT**	**240**	**6–2**	**Sr**
Howell, Carroll	LH	171	5–9	Sr
Keller, John	LT	210	6–0	So
Krisher, Jerry	RT	230	6–0	Sr
Kriss, Frederick	RE	193	5–11	So
Leggett, David	**QB**	**192**	**6–1**	**Sr**

Lilienthal, Robert	QB	174	6–0	So
Ludwig, Paul	RE	208	6–3	Jr
Machinsky, Francis	**RT**	**212**	**6–0**	**Jr**
Michael, William	LE	204	6–1	So
Nussbaum, Lee	FB	212	6–1	So
Okulovich, Andrew	QB	187	5–11	So
Parker, Jim	**LG**	**248**	**6–3**	**So**
Quinn, Thomas	LG	190	5–10	So
Ramser, Richard	LG	191	5–11	Jr
Reichenbach, James	**RG**	**200**	**5–10**	**Sr**
Riticher, Raymond	RG	198	5–10	Sr
Roseboro, James	RH	173	5–9	So
Shedd, Jan	RH	173	5–10	Jr
Shingledecker, William	RE	181	5–10	So
Slicker, Richard	C	193	6–3	So
Sommers, Karl	C	215	6–2	So
Spears, Thomas	RE	193	6–0	Jr
Stoeckel, Donald	LT	214	6–0	Jr
Swartz, Donald	LT	226	6–1	Sr
Theis, Franklyn	QB	195	5–10	So
Thomas, Aurealius	RT	197	6–1	Fr
Thompson, Kenneth	RH	184	6–0	So
Thornton, Robert	C	192	6–0	Sr
Trabue, Jerry	LE	203	6–3	So
Vargo, Kenneth	**C**	**192**	**6–1**	**Jr**
Verhoff, Jack	RT	250	6–4	Jr
Vicic, Donald	FB	209	6–1	So
Wassmund, James	LG	200	6–0	So
Watkins, Robert	**RH**	**196**	**5–9**	**Sr**
Weaver, David	LG	191	5–8	Jr
Weed, Thurlow	K	151	5–5	Sr
Williams, David	RG	206	6–0	Sr
Williams, Lee	LH	174	5–10	So
Young, James	FB	192	6–0	So
Young, Richard	RH	168	5–10	Sr

1957

9–1

(Includes 10–7 Rose Bowl victory over Oregon.
National champions in UPI poll)
Woody Hayes, head coach

	Pos.	Ht.	Wt.	Yr.
Anders, Richard	LG	180	5–8	So
Arnold, Birtho	RT	269	6–2	So
Bailey, Ralph	RG	198	6–0	Jr
Baldacci, Thomas	RG	200	6–0	Sr
Ballinger, Gerry	LH	178	5–10	Jr
Ballmer, Paul	QB	186	5–10	Jr
Beam, William	C	197	6–1	So
Beerman, Raymond	LH	191	5–11	Sr
Bowermaster, Russell	LE	202	6–2	Jr
Bowsher, Gerald	LG	198	5–10	Jr
Breehl, Edward	C	192	6–0	Sr
Brown, Leo (co-captain)	**RE**	**171**	**5–10**	**Sr**
Bryant, Eugene	LT	222	6–2	So
Cannavino, Joseph	LH	172	5–11	Sr
Carr, Leroy	RH	186	6–1	So
Cisco, Galen (co-captain)	FB	203	5–11	Sr
Clark, Donald	**LH**	**191**	**5–11**	**Jr**
Cook, Ronald	RT	204	6–1	Sr
Cowans, Leroy	RG	207	5–10	So
Crawford, Albert	LT	228	6–0	Jr
Crawford, Thomas	QB	178	5–11	Sr
Crowl, Don	C	216	5–11	So
Disher, Larry	RE	182	5–11	Sr
Dresser, John	RH	192	6–1	So
Fields, Jerry	C	206	6–1	So
Frank, Daniel	C	189	5–11	Jr
Gage, Ralph	FB	174	5–10	Jr
Houston, James	**LE**	**216**	**6–2**	**So**

James, Daniel	**C**	**258**	**6–2**	**Jr**
Jobko, William	**LG**	**212**	**6–1**	**Sr**
Jones, Herbert	LG	192	5–10	Sr
Katula, Theodore	LE	193	6–1	Sr
Kilgore, David	PK	160	5–9	So
Kreakbaum, Thomas	LT	233	6–0	So
Kremblas, Frank	**QB**	**198**	**6–1**	**Jr**
LeBeau, Dick	**LH**	**183**	**6–0**	**Jr**
Lord, John	LE	177	5–10	Jr
Marshall, Jim	**RT**	**232**	**6–3**	**So**
Martin, John	RT	214	5–11	Sr
Matz, James	RT	222	6–0	So
McMurray, Preston	RH	178	5–9	Jr
Michael, Richard	LE	221	6–2	So
Moran, John	RH	186	5–10	So
Morgan, Thomas	RE	202	6–2	Jr
Nagy, Alex	LT	230	6–2	Sr
Okulovich, Andy	QB	188	5–11	Jr
Provenza, Russell	FB	186	5–11	Sr
Robinson, Philip	RH	176	5–9	Jr
Rowland, James	LE	200	6–4	So
Samuels, James	QB	186	6–0	So
Schafrath, Dick	**LT**	**216**	**6–2**	**Jr**
Schenking, Fred	RE	206	6–4	Jr
Schram, Bruce	RT	206	6–0	So
Seilkop, Kenneth	LT	202	5–11	So
Spychalski, Ernest	RG	248	6–2	Jr
Sutherin, Donald	K	194	5–11	Sr
Thomas, Aurealius	**RG**	**204**	**6–1**	**Sr**
Trivisonno, Joseph	FB	214	5–11	Sr
Vitatoe, Ronald	QB	186	6–0	So
Wagner, David	LT	234	6–2	So
Wentz, William	LH	176	5–11	So
White, Bob	**FB**	**207**	**6–2**	**So**
Zawacki, Charles	RE	208	6–2	Sr
Zuhars, David	LH	178	6–1	So

1968

10–0

(Includes 27–16 Rose Bowl win
over Southern California.
Consensus national champions)
Woody Hayes, head coach

	Pos.	Ht.	Wt.	Yr.
Douglas Adams	**LB**	**6–0**	**215**	**So**
Charles Aldrin	E	6–3	207	So
Tim Anderson	**CB**	**6–0**	**194**	**So**
Daniel Aston	DE	6–2	208	Jr
Tom Backhus	**G**	**5–11**	**207**	**Jr**
Thomas Bartley	LB	5–11	198	Sr
Edward Bender	RHB	6–0	172	Sr
Jay Bombach	RHB	6–1	201	Sr
John Brockington	**RHB**	**6–1**	**210**	**So**
David Brungard	LHB	5–10	184	Jr
Arthur Burton	LB	6–1	193	Jr
David Cheney	G	6–3	230	So
James Coburn	DB	5–11	190	So
James Conroy	OG	6–2	208	So
Steven Crapser	DT	6–1	216	Jr
Dick Cunningham	FB	5–10	188	So
Mark Debevc	**DE**	**6–1**	**210**	**So**
John Dombos	DT	6–0	205	So
Brian Donovan	G	6–3	206	So
Thomas Ecrement	DE	6–0	195	So
Gerald Ehrsam	S	6–0	194	Sr
David Foley (co-captain)	**RT**	**6–5**	**246**	**Sr**
James Gentile	LB	6–2	210	Jr
Ray Gillian	LHB	5–11	194	Jr
Horatius Greene	LHB	5–11	180	Jr
William Hackett	LB	6–1	204	Jr
Randy Hart	RT	6–2	220	Jr
Leophus Hayden	LHB	6–2	204	So
Ralph Holloway	MG	6–1	222	So
Paul Huff	FB	6–3	217	Jr
Charles Hutchison	LT	6–3	240	Jr
Alan Jack	**RG**	**6–0**	**215**	**Jr**
Bruce Jankowski	**E**	**5–11**	**192**	**So**
Rex Kern	**QB**	**6–0**	**180**	**So**
Gerald King	DE	6–3	208	So

Richard Kuhn	RE	6–2	208	So
Ted Kurz	G	6–2	222	So
Edward Lapuh	DE	6–1	198	So
Billy Long	QB	6–1	180	Sr
Ron Maciejowski	QB	6–2	186	So
Jack Marsh	DE	6–2	208	So
Rufus Mayes	**LT**	**6–5**	**250**	**Sr**
Dick Merryman	K	5–8	175	Jr
John Muhlbach	**C**	**5–10**	**194**	**Sr**
Brad Nielsen	**DT**	**6–3**	**222**	**Jr**
Jim Oppermann	LT	6–4	240	So
Jim Otis	**FB**	**6–0**	**208**	**Jr**
Steven Page	S	5–10	176	So
Mike Polaski	DB	5–10	170	Jr
Bill Pollitt	LB	6–2	212	Jr
Ted Provost	**DB**	**6–3**	**182**	**Jr**
Larry Qualls	C	6–0	190	So
Richard Quilling	S	6–1	190	Jr
Michael Radtke	LB	6–1	200	Jr
Jim Roman	C/K	6–0	211	Sr
Nick Roman	DE	6–4	221	Sr
Gary Roush	RT	6–4	200	Sr
Kevin Rusnak	RHB	6–1	190	Jr
Paul Schmidlin	**DT**	**6–1**	**222**	**Jr**
Mike Sensibaugh	**S/P**	**6–0**	**187**	**So**
Bruce Smith	S	5–10	150	So
Butch Smith	DT	6–2	224	Jr
Robert Smith	RE	6–4	221	Sr
John Sobolewski	DE	6–1	192	Sr
Mark Stier	**LB**	**6–1**	**202**	**Sr**
Jim Stillwagon	**MG**	**6–0**	**220**	**So**
Vic Stottlemyer	MG	6–0	200	Sr
John Stowe	LE	6–2	200	Sr
Phil Strickland	G	6–1	217	So
Vince Suber	LB	6–1	186	So
Jack Tatum	**CB**	**6–0**	**204**	**So**
Robert Trapuzzano	DB	6–0	187	Jr
Richard Troha	RT	6–3	227	So
Bill Urbanik	DT	6–3	238	Sr
Tim Wagner	DB	5–10	175	So
Charles Waugh	G	6–0	180	So
Jan White	**LE**	**6–2**	**214**	**So**
David Whitfield	**DE**	**6–0**	**184**	**Jr**
Dirk Worden (co-captain)	LB	6–0	198	Sr
Larry Zelina	**WB**	**6–0**	**195**	**So**

2002

14–0

(Includes 31–24 double-overtime victory over Miami in Fiesta Bowl, setting NCAA Division I-A record for most wins in a season. Consensus national champions)

Jim Tressel, head coach

	Pos.	Ht.	Wt.	Yr.
John Adams	FB	6–11	210	So
Will Allen	FS	6–2	190	Jr
Tim Anderson	DT	6–4	289	Jr
David Andrews	TE	6–2	225	So
Kyle Andrews	LS	5–11	245	So
Reggie Arden	TE	6–4	240	Fr
Bryce Bishop	**OG**	**6–3**	**312**	**Jr**
Mike Bogart	OG	6–3	290	Jr
Jason Bond	LB	6–3	240	Jr
Le Andre Boone	FS	6–1	195	Fr
Joe Bradley	LB	6–3	213	Fr
Bobby Britton	CB	5–11	194	Jr
Jason Caldwell	TE	6–5	265	So
Bobby Carpenter	LB	6–3	240	Fr
Drew Carter	SE	6–4	200	Jr
Angelo Chattams	FL	5–11	185	So
Bam Childress	FL	5–9	180	So
Maurice Clarett	**TB**	**6–0**	**230**	**Fr**
Adrien Clarke	**OG**	**6–5**	**325**	**Jr**
R.J. Coleman	TE	6–5	265	Fr
John Conroy	OL	6–3	275	Fr
Chris Conwell	CB	5–10	190	Sr
Ryan Cook	OT	6–7	305	Fr
Bryce Culver	DE	6–4	217	So
Mike D'Andrea	LB	6–3	240	Fr
Doug Datish	OT	6–5	290	Fr
Michael DeMaria	TB	5–9	170	So
Mike Doss	**SS**	**5–11**	**204**	**Sr**
Ivan Douglas	OT	6–8	305	Jr
T.J. Downing	OL	6–5	280	Fr
Tyler Everett	DB	6–1	185	Fr
Dustin Fox	**CB**	**6–0**	**190**	**So**

Simon Fraser	DE	6–6	250	So
Chris Gamble	**FL/CB**	**6–2**	**180**	**So**
Steve Graef	DE	6–2	240	So
Cie Grant	**LB**	**6–1**	**220**	**Sr**
Marcus Green	DT	6–3	300	Fr
Andy Groom	**P/H**	**6–1**	**185**	**Sr**
Maurice Hall	TB	5–10	190	So
Roy Hall	WR	6–3	210	Fr
Ryan Hamby	TE	6–5	240	Fr
Rob Harley	DB	6–2	202	So
Ben Hartsock	**TE**	**6–4**	**264**	**Jr**
A.J. Hawk	LB	6–2	230	Fr
John Hollins	SE	6–2	180	So
Santonio Holmes	WR	5–11	170	Fr
Andre Hooks	WR	6–2	205	So
Josh Huston	PK	6–1	195	So
Harlen Jacobs	CB	6–1	197	So
Michael Jenkins	**SE**	**6–5**	**200**	**Jr**
Branden Joe	**FB**	**6–0**	**245**	**So**
Jesse Kline	RB	6–1	227	Jr
Mike Kne	OT	6–4	205	Jr
Craig Kolk	WR	6–1	192	Fr
Craig Krenzel	**QB**	**6–4**	**215**	**Jr**
Mike Kudla	DE	6–3	235	Fr
Scott Kuhnhein	OG	6–4	285	Sr
Maurice Lee	FL	5–9	178	Jr
Jamel Luke	WR	5–11	175	Jr
Nick Mangold	OL	6–4	270	Fr
Thomas Matthews	SS	6–2	210	So
John McLaughlin	OT	6–6	290	So
Scott McMullen	QB	6–3	215	Jr
Richard McNutt	CB	5–11	178	Jr
Jeremy Miller	LS	5–10	200	Jr
Brandon Mitchell	DB	6–3	190	Fr
Aaron Mochon	RB	6–3	245	Fr
Steven Moore	CB	5–10	185	So
Derek Morris	OT	6–6	350	Fr
Ben Nash	OL	6–3	275	Fr
Donnie Nickey	**FS**	**6–3**	**203**	**Sr**
Mike Nugent	**PK**	**5–10**	**170**	**So**
Adam Olds	OG	6–5	275	Fr
Shane Olives	**OT**	**6–5**	**310**	**Jr**

Pat O'Neill	LB	6–3	230	Jr
Jim Otis	QB	5–10	200	So
Fred Pagac Jr.	LB	6–1	225	Jr
Roshawn Parker	RB	5–11	219	Jr
Steve Pavelka	RB	5–7	165	So
Joel Penton	DE	6–5	255	Fr
Kenny Peterson	**DT**	**6–4**	**265**	**Sr**
Scott Petroff	WR	5–11	180	Jr
Quinn Pitcock	DL	6–4	285	Fr
Robert Reynolds	**LB**	**6–3**	**234**	**Jr**
Jay Richardson	DE	6–5	245	Fr
JaJa Riley	TB	6–2	205	Fr
Mike Roberts	CB	5–11	178	Fr
Lydell Ross	TB	6–0	210	So
Matt Russell	K	5–11	184	Sr
Nate Salley	DB	6–3	180	Fr
B.J. Sander	P	6–3	212	Jr
Tim Schafer	DE	6–5	250	Fr
Brandon Schnittker	FB	6–1	250	Fr
Darrion Scott	**DE**	**6–3**	**271**	**Jr**
Rob Sims	OL	6–4	290	Fr
Troy Smith	QB	6–1	205	Fr
Will Smith	**DE**	**6–4**	**250**	**Jr**
Michael Stafford	OT	6–3	280	Sr
Nate Stead	FB	6–0	250	Jr
Alex Stepanovich	**C**	**6–4**	**310**	**Jr**
David Thompson	DT	6–5	290	Sr
Matt Trombitas	QB	6–5	224	Fr
Jack Tucker	FB	6–1	235	Sr
Kyle Turano	P/K	6–0	195	Jr
Andree Tyree	C	6–3	280	Fr
E.J. Underwood	DB	6–1	175	Fr
Chris Vance	FL	6–2	180	Sr
Bryan Weaver	P/DB	5–10	196	So
Stan White Jr.	LB	6–3	230	Fr
Kurt Wilhelm	LS	6–0	230	So
Matt Wilhelm	**LB**	**6–5**	**245**	**Sr**
Sam Williams	DL	6–3	237	So
Steve Winner	OL	6–6	270	Fr
Mike Young	WR	6–5	205	So
Justin Zwick	QB	6–4	210	Fr

BIBLIOGRAPHY

Associated Press. "Michigan Defeats Ohio State, 9 to 3." *New York Times*: 26 Nov. 1950, S1.

Borst, Bill. *Ohio State Football Trivia*. Boston, Mass.: Quinlan Press, 1988.

Buchanan, Lamont. *The Story of Football*. New York City: The Vanguard Press. Inc., 1952.

Buck, Jack with Rob Rains, Bob Broeg. *Jack Buck: "That's a Winner!"* Champaign, Ill.: Sagamore Publishing, 1997.

Cohen, Richard M. and Jordan A. Deutsch, David S. Neft. *The Ohio State Football Scrapbook*. Indianapolis, Ind.: Bobbs-Merrill Company, Inc., 1977.

Emmanuel, Greg. *The 100-Yard War: Inside the 100-Year-Old Michigan-Ohio State Football Rivalry*. Hoboken, N.J.: John Wiley & Sons, Inc., 2004.

Greenberg, Steve and Larry Zelina. *Ohio State '68: All the Way to the Top*. Champaign, Ill.: Sports Publishing Inc., 1998.

Harper, William L. *An Ohio State Man: Esco Sarkkinen Remembers OSU Football*. Marble Hill, Ga.: Enthea Press, 2000.

Homan, Marvin and Paul Hornung. *Ohio State: 100 Years of Football* [Special Centennial Ed.]. Columbus, Ohio: The Ohio State University, 1990.

Hooley, Bruce, et al. *Greatest Moments in Ohio State Football History*. Chicago: Triumph Books, 2003.

Hornung, Paul. *The Best of the Buckeyes*. Columbus, Ohio: Zimmerman & Leonard, Inc., 1982.

Kaelin, Eric. *Buckeye Glory Days: The Most Memorable Games of Ohio State Football*. Sports Publishing LLC, 2004.

Keels, Paul. *Paul Keels's Tales from the Buckeyes' Championship Season*. Sports Publishing LLC, 2003.

Keys, Tom. *The Battling Buckeyes*. Worthington, Ohio: Education Associates, Inc., 1975.

Leckie, Robert. *The Story of Football*. New York: Random House, Inc., 1965.

Levy, Bill. *Three Yards and a Cloud of Dust: The Ohio State Football Story*. Cleveland, Ohio: The World Publishing Company, 1966.

Maddux, Jason, ed. *Mission Accomplished: A Perfect Season*.

Columbus, Ohio: Newspaper Network of Central Ohio, 2003.

Murphy, Austin. "Mighty Mo: Precocious freshman tailback Maurice Clarett made his presence felt—on and off the field." *Sports Illustrated Presents Ohio State Buckeyes: 2002 National Champions, Commemorative Issue, 2003*: 15–17.

Murray, Jim and Arthur Daley, William N. Wallace, et al. *The Heisman: Sixty Years of Tradition and Excellence.* Bronxville, N.Y.: Adventure Quest, Inc., 1995.

Natali, Alan. *Woody's Boys: 20 Famous Buckeyes Talk Amongst Themselves.* Wilmington, Ohio: Orange Frazer Press, 1995.

Park, Jack. *Ohio State Football: The Great Tradition.* Columbus, Ohio: Lexington Press, 1992.

Rapp, Jeff. *Stadium Stories: Ohio State Buckeyes—Colorful Tales of the Scarlet and Gray.* Guilford, Conn.: The Globe Pequot Press, 2003.

Skipton, Todd W. *A Shot at a Rose, To the Bite of a Gator: The '75-'78 Ohio State Football Saga.* Columbus, Ohio: The Brawny Pug Publishing Co., 1993.

Snapp, Steve, ed. *Ohio State 2004 Football Media Guide.* Columbus, Ohio: The Ohio State Athletic Communications Office, 2004.

Snook, Jeff. *A Buckeye Season: The Inside Story of the Glory and Heartbreak of Ohio State's 1995 Season.* Indianapolis, Ind.: Masters Press, 1996.

Snypp, Wilbur and Bob Hunter. *The Buckeyes: A Story of Ohio State Football.* Tomball, Texas: The Strode Publishers, 1988.

Taylor, Phil. "Undefeated . . . 'Nuff Said." *Sports Illustrated Presents Ohio State Buckeyes: 2002 National Champions, Commemorative Issue, 2003*: 10–11.

Tressel, Jim; Jeff Snook, ed. *What It Means to Be a Buckeye.* Chicago: Triumph Books, 2003.

Vancil, Mark, ed. *ABC Sports College Football All-Time All-America Team.* New York: Hyperion, 2000.

Weigel, J. Timothy. *The Buckeyes: Ohio State Football.* Chicago: Henry Regnery Company, 1974.

Wentz, Howard E. *Touchdown Buckeyes: My Days with the Ohio State Buckeyes.* Defiance, Ohio: S/B Publications, 1984.

Whittingham, Richard. *Rites of Autumn: The Story of College Football.* New York: The Free Press, 2001.

WEBSITES

www.newsday.com/sports/print edition/ ny-spnu-gent244273998may24,0,7073449.story?coll=ny-sports-print

http://sports.espn.go.com/ncf/recap?gameId=243250194&confId=null

INDEX

INDEX